Sister Teresa Margaret McCarthy with Sandra Counahan

This book is dedicated to
Ralph and Sister Teresa Margaret McCarthy

For the encouragment Sister has given all her pupils over the years and
for passing on to us a love of Mountmellick Work, we thank her.

TRADITIONAL IRISH EMBROIDERY

MOUNTMELLICK WORK

Redrawn from Pim patterns

DETAIL FROM ANTIQUE LINEN QUILT

TRADITIONAL IRISH EMBROIDERY

MOUNTMELLICK WORK

SANDRA COUNAHAN

Redrawn from
Pim patterns

DETAIL FROM ANTIQUE LINEN QUILT

THE NEEDLE-WOMAN'S PRAYER

God grant that I may see the stitch

until my dying day

and when my last short thread is clipped

and scissors tucked away

the work that I have done live on

that other folk may see

the pleasure I have known Lord

in the skill you gave to me

Anon.

Redrawn from Pim patterns

MERCIER PRESS
Douglas Village, Cork
Email: books@mercierpress.ie
Website: www.mercierpress.ie

Trade enquiries to CMD Distribution
55A Spruce Avenue, Stillorgan Industrial Park
Blackrock, County Dublin
Tel: (01) 294 2560; Fax: (01) 294 2564
E-mail: cmd@columba.ie

Photography by John O'Neill LRPS
All photographs are © Glass Image Photography Studios, 2005, www.glassimage.ie

ISBN 185635 485 7

10 9 8 7 6 5 4 3 2 1

A CIP record for this title is available from the British Library

Cover: work from pattern in Weldons, 8th Series

Patterns may be reproduced for personal use only

SUPPORTED BY THE HERITAGE COUNCIL

LE CUIDIÚ AN CHOMHAIRLE OIDHREACHTA

This publication has received support
from the Heritage Council under the
2005 Publications Grant Scheme

Mercier Press receives financial assistance from
the Arts Council/An Chomhairle Ealaíon

Printed in Ireland by ColourBooks Ltd

CONTENTS

Note: Superscript numbers throughout the book denote sources in the Notes section on page 128

DETAIL FROM ANTIQUE LINEN QUILT

INTRODUCTION

Irish traditional needlework, i.e. Sprigging, Flowering and Mountmellick Work, has tended to consist of white stitching on white cloth using designs taken from nature.

However, Mountmellick Work is textured by a wide variety of stitches and bold designs which compensate for the lack of colour. It is an embroidery of great richness and elegance.

The variety of stitches is the joy of the work, and the diversity of designs gives great scope for the imagination. As the work is heavy small open spaces are left between the elements to produce the necessary balance so essential to an artistic piece of embroidery.

All stitches can have your own variation on them; the antique pieces are full of it. Any stitch can be used in any situation, although studying the antique pieces it is Satin Stitch which is used mainly for the dog rose, Bullion for wheat and French Knots on blackberries. Some stitches are also unique to Mountmellick Work, such as Snail Trail, Thorn, Cable Plait and Indian Filler.

Sister Teresa Margaret, who revived the embroidery, no longer travels to teach but continues her interest in the craft. We owe her a great debt of gratitude. I will always be grateful for her patience and kind words of encouragement at my first lesson and since.

TABLECLOTH
CORNER UNIT

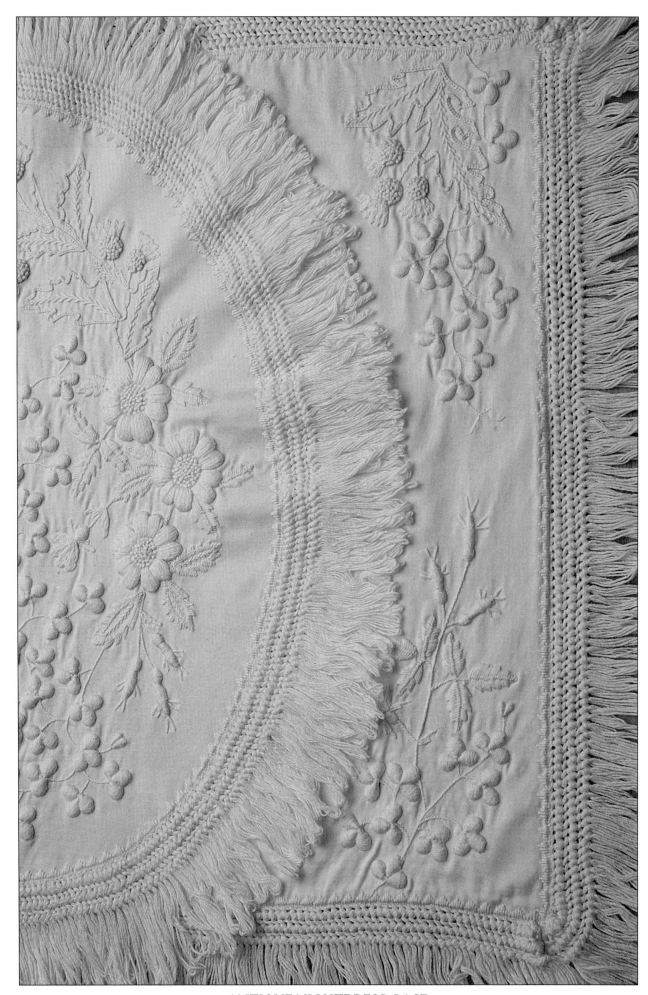

ANTIQUE NIGHTDRESS CASE

ACKNOWLEDGEMENTS

Thanks to:
Gavin and Guy Counahan
Pat O'Donnell
Avril and Aubrey Lang
Terry Concannon
Barbara Yoder
Máirín Dunne
Barbara Rossell
Joan O'Donoghue
The National Museum of Ireland

Photographs:
Glass Image Photography

Illustrator:
Frances Counahan
Sandra Counahan

Modern examples worked by:
Veronica Davis
Linda O'Keeffe
Chris Cleary
Joan O'Donoghue
Tilly Roche
Stasia Hayes
Noreen Roche
Margaret McKeown
Sandra Counahan
Margaret Healy

Antique examples:
Miss C. Grubb
Breda Walsh
Sandra Counahan
An Grianan Adult Education College

Patterns:
Redrawn from Pim collection
(with permission of Mountmellick
Museum Committee)
Phil O'Rourke
Sandra Counahan

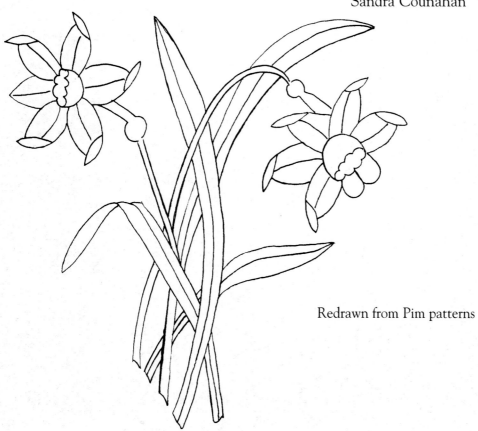

Redrawn from Pim patterns

ANTIQUE BRUSH & COMB BAG

CHARACTERISTICS of
MOUNTMELLICK WORK

1. It is worked on a white, heavy, satinised cotton jean. The fabric we use today is manufactured for the upholstery industry and for dyeing and/or artwork.

2. A variety of thicknesses of white matt cotton thread are used, up to and including 4ply knitting cotton.

3. The stitching is both fine and heavy on the same piece. Padded stitching is used to raise the height of the stitch, as are two different stitches on top of each other.

4. There is no turned-in hem, the packed Buttonhole Stitch must be worked on all pieces as this forms the hem. The raw edge of the fabric will fray back over time to the Buttonholing but not beyond.

5. There is a knitted, uncut fringe.

6. There are no eyelets or cut work.

7. When using filler stitches you do not have to follow nature's lines.

8. The pieces have large bold designs.

9. The material is well covered with embroidery, Scattering is used when the pattern has open spaces as part of the design.

10. Natural flora and the seashore are the inspiration for the patterns.

11. Leaves obey no law of nature except in outline, each group being embroidered differently.

Pattern from antique sampler

DETAIL ON ANTIQUE QUILT

HISTORY

Mountmellick Work is thought to have been invented by Mrs Johanna Carter in the town of Mountmellick in Ireland in 1825–30.[12] Mrs Carter lived in an age when ladies of her social standing were taught painting, sketching and embroidery to fill their days. So, taking her inspiration from the banks of the river Owenass that flows through the town, she transferred her skills into bold designs for embroidery. The embroidery was based on Crewel wool work and some stitches she invented herself. She is recorded as having run a small school for girls in the town and embroidery would have been one of the subjects taught. The town at the time had a thriving linen and cotton industry with milling, spinning and weaving. Times were getting hard however and famine was looming. Mrs Carter, like other women of her class, tried to help the poor and used the available local materials of white cotton and thread to teach the local women her unique style of embroidery. She set up a cottage industry to sell the items these women made. There are records of items of Mountmellick Work having been sold to the gentry of the day. This cottage industry lasted only a few years; we have no records to tell why it failed or what happened to Mrs Carter. This gave us the first decline of the embroidery.

In 1880, Mrs Millner, a member of the Religious Society of Friends [Quakers] started The Industrial Association in order to help distressed 'Irish gentlewomen' in Mountmellick whose financial circumstances had been affected by the famines.[13] Ten years later, in 1890, the association had fifty workers employed in a most successful business selling Mrs Carter's style of embroidery. It was at this time the embroidery got its name of Mountmellick Work. By now, the embroidery was becoming a social pastime for ladies throughout the British Isles and in North America, due to the publication of embroidery booklets in both places.[1] The first edition of Weldons booklets on the subject said that the embroidery was being taught in schools in the town and was being carried out extensively in the neighbourhood under the auspices of the association.[16] In 1882, the Presentation Sisters in Mountmellick were teaching the embroidery to the girls in their primary school. They also held an exhibition in Dublin of work they themselves had done in the hope of generating enough demand to employ the poor girls of the town in the association also. By 1907 however, interest in the embroidery had waned and the numbers employed by the association had fallen to eight. By the start of the First World War in 1914 the second decline had set in.

The members of the Quaker community in Ireland continued to do the embroidery both at home and in their schools as it appealed to their ethos of not using flamboyant colours. The tradition in the Quaker boarding schools was to make personal items for their own use and their future daughters, and also household items for what is called the 'bottom drawer'.[12] During the early years of the boarding school in Mountmellick the girls made items of embroidery for sale to help pay for their textbooks. In later years it became a tradition for the members of the Friends to give pieces of the embroidery as gifts and never to sell it. In the early 1900s the pupil numbers had fallen in the Quaker school and the embroidery was no longer taught. The school closed in 1920 and was bought by the Presentation Sisters who continued to run it as a girls' school.

In 1948, the nuns were still teaching Mountmellick Work but even at this time it was dying out. Sister Teresa Margaret McCarthy, a retired nun in the convent, was asked in the early 1970s by a local historian for information about the embroidery and this started its current rise in popularity. Having found some patterns in the convent (a gift from a prominent Quaker family, the Pims) and, using examples of work from other families, Sister taught herself the craft. She held classes in the town and soon nationwide until prevented from doing so recently by ill health. Today the craft enjoys worldwide popularity and, in the town of Mountmellick, a museum dedicated to it is now open.

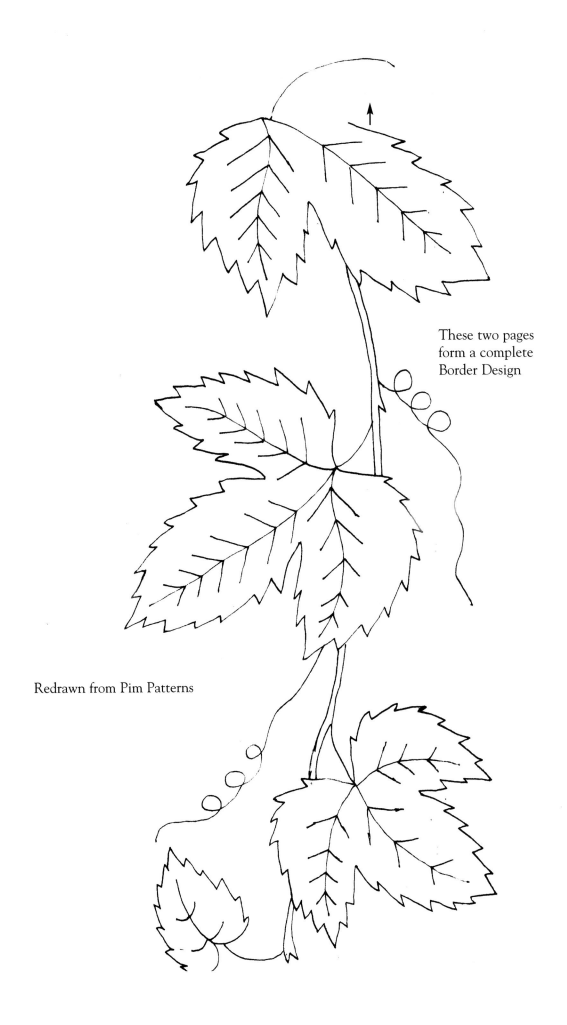

These two pages
form a complete
Border Design

Redrawn from Pim Patterns

Getting Started

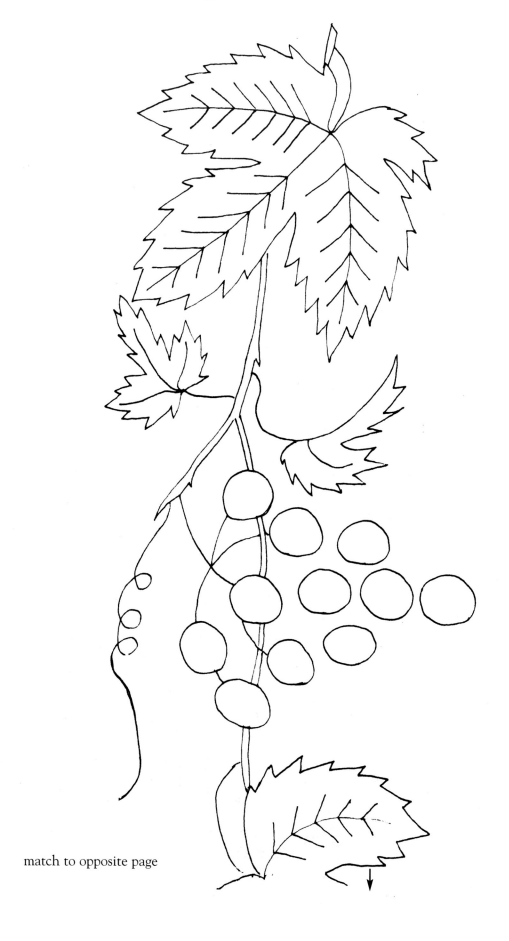

match to opposite page

DETAIL ON ANTIQUE QUILT

MATERIALS and EQUIPMENT

Heavy white cotton satin
White matt cotton thread
Sewing needles
Scissors
Ruler
Embroidery ring
Masking tape
Greaseproof paper
Embroidery pen or pencil

Cotton buds
Black fine tip pen
Light box
Patterns
Thimble
Coloured knitting cotton (see Fringes)
Knitting needles (see Fringes)
Empty cotton reel (see Fringes)

HEAVY WHITE COTTON SATIN

This cotton is cream in colour before washing, and comes in a width of 137cm. The fabric needs to be heavy to take the weight of the embroidery and the thickness of thread used. One side is rough in texture and the other is smooth to the touch, hence the word satin [pronounced sateen]. TAKE CARE when placing the pattern that it goes on the smooth side.

WHITE MATT COTTON THREAD

The threads used vary in size from fine to thick. Some of the cotton is sold as mercerised (with a shine) but the shine is very light and dulls after boiling (see laundry). A large amount of thread is used in the embroidery, especially in knitting the fringe. 50gm balls of cotton for crochet and fine knitting can be used; look for a thread that is not fluffy and whose twist is smooth. A 4ply cotton used for knitted garments is suitable for padding on the large elements of a design.

SEWING NEEDLES

A range of needles are required: Chenille, which are sharp and have a large eye are for general stitching (both the thick ones and the thin are used as each will give a different appearance to the stitch); Tapestry, which are needed for whipping and the larger ones, with an eye that will take three or four threads, for grafting the fringe; thick and thin Darning needles are used for long Bullion Knots.

TAPESTRY   CHENILLE   DARNING

THICK

THREAD   MEDIUM

THIN

ANTIQUE SIDEBOARD COVER

SCISSORS

I use straight nail scissors as they are very sharp, have a fine point, are inexpensive and can be thrown out when blunt and a new pair bought.

RULER

A 15cm clear plastic ruler is a must when drawing lines for something like a trellis: you can see the underlying design and therefore judge the position correctly.

EMBROIDERY RING

I use a 15cm flexible plastic ring, which is sold for displaying embroidery and has a removable hook at the top. It gives very good tension to the fabric and is large enough for the small area I wish to work on at any one time. Remove the ring on completion of work and never leave the ring on overnight.

MASKING TAPE

Decorator's masking tape is used to attach the pattern and the fabric to the light box as it will not damage the paper and fabric when it is peeled off.

GREASEPROOF or TRACING PAPER

Draw and trace the patterns on to this paper. They can then be photocopied as a permanent record. Do not use parchment baking paper or freezer paper as the ink can smudge on them.

EMBROIDERY PEN or PENCIL

If using a water soluble pen use only the blue as the red one does not always disappear; the same applies to dressmakers' carbon which can be quite messy to use for embroidery. The water soluble pen line can be removed using a damp cotton bud and the line adjusted to suit the stitching as you work. The Royal School of Needlework at present does not recommend the use of water soluble pens as it is not known what effect these chemicals will have on the fabric in the long term. If left exposed to light or heat the blue will fade and leave a yellow stain, so never iron your work while the design is on it or leave it sitting exposed when not working on it. To remove any such stains see the laundry chapter. The pattern on antique pieces was put on with pencil. Use a hard lead, B or HB and you will find that this can be rubbed out with an eraser and washed out.

COTTON BUDS

Baby cotton buds and water are used to sponge off small areas when re-adjusting patterns drawn with a water soluble pen.

BLACK FINE TIP PEN

Never use a felt or ballpoint pen to draw your designs on paper. If you use a light box, the heat can cause the ink to come off onto the fabric. I use a Stabilo, which is a fine-tipped ink pen; mechanical drawing pens are also suitable.

Redrawn from Weldons
3rd series

13

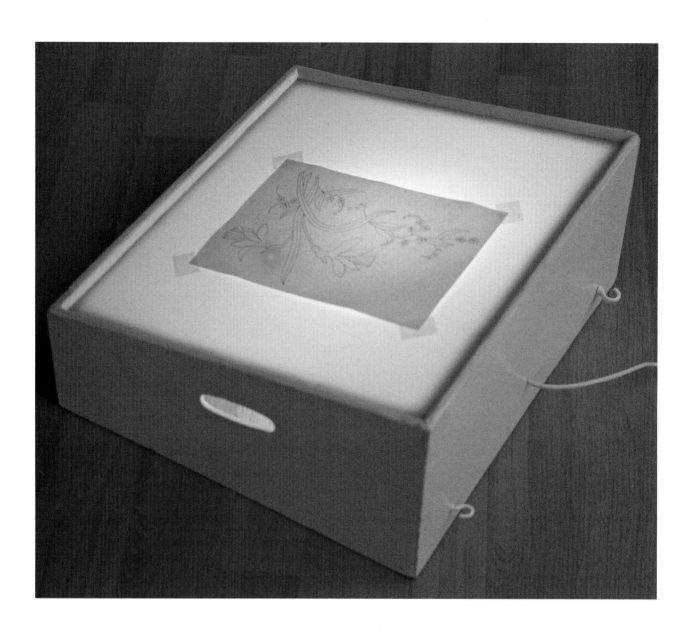

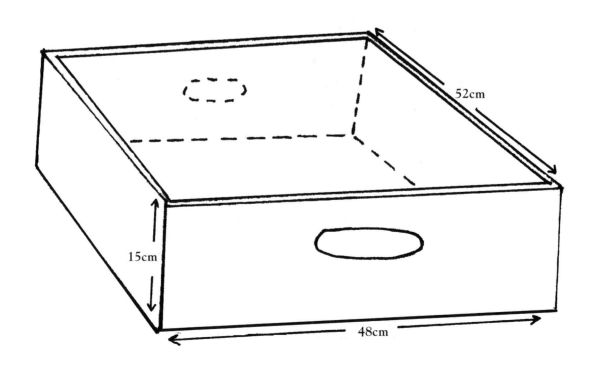

52cm

15cm

48cm

14

LIGHT BOX

A large light box is required for Mountmellick Work; mine is homemade with a white Perspex top, which is safer than glass. There must be ventilation for the heat generated by the light bulb and this forms a carrying handle. The bulb socket is screwed to the back wall of the box. I use a long life bulb as it doesn't generate as much heat as the standard bulb. Two hooks on the outside allow the cord to be stored. The top slopes, making it more comfortable to work on. An old drawer is a good alternative base for your light box. A small table turned upside down with a table lamp, minus the shade and a sheet of Perspex balanced on the legs will also work nearly as well.

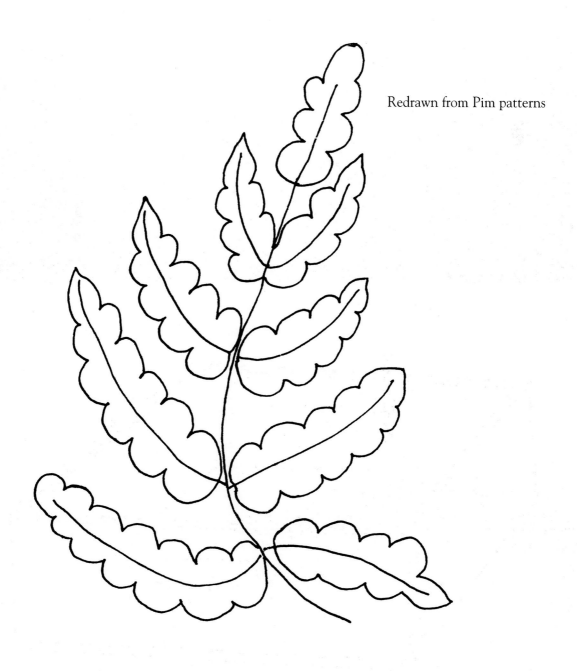

Redrawn from Pim patterns

ANTIQUE PATTERN from PIM COLLECTION

PATTERNS

In the early 1900s patterns were available to buy from some publishers of needlework magazines such as Weldons and Briggs in England and Penelope in America. The antique patterns now in the Mountmellick museum however are thought to be homemade, and it is from copies of these that we work. The metal engravings of patterns and pieces in the old periodicals can be drawn out and used by first photocopying, enlarging and then tracing them off onto greaseproof or tracing paper.

Drawn elements appear in this book and can be enlarged if required and used to make your own designs. Straight runs of patterns can be turned into circles and the elements on any pattern can be repositioned.

Mountmellick patterns differ from other floral designs in that the elements seldom overlap, maybe just a leaf tip behind a petal, but generally the unit is complete in itself. Taking patterns from antique items of embroidery is simple: just photocopy the piece and trace the image onto grease-proof or tracing paper. If the piece is too large to photocopy, tape the paper using masking tape to the item and trace over the design with a pencil. (Never use a pen for this tracing, the ink could go through onto the fabric.) Having removed the tracing from the fabric, redefine the pattern with the ink pen. A permanent photocopy of all patterns should always be made as the greaseproof paper goes brittle with time.

Always think of the pattern as a guide to the shape you want, it is not an embroidery design where you are using a permanent transfer which must be covered. This is a style of embroidery where you are in charge and you can make as many alterations to the pattern as often as you like. No design is difficult, it just depends on the variety of stitches you use. Some antique pieces would only have five or six different stitches in total.

Redrawn from Pim patterns

17

ANTIQUE DOILY

ELEMENTS USED in DESIGNS

Acorn and Oak Leaf	Fern	Pansy
Bindweed	Forget-Me-Not	Passion Flower
Bird	Fuchsia	Seaweed
Blackberry	Harp *[represents Ireland]*	Sea-Shell
Butterfly	Honeysuckle	Shamrock *[represents Ireland]*
Clover	Hop	Strawberry
Cyclamen	Ivy	Thistle *[represents Scotland]*
Daisy	Lily	Vine and Grape
Dog Rose and Hips *[represents England]*	Monogram	Virginia Creeper
Elderberry	Mountain Ash (Leaf and Berry)	Wheat
Family Crest	Narcissus	

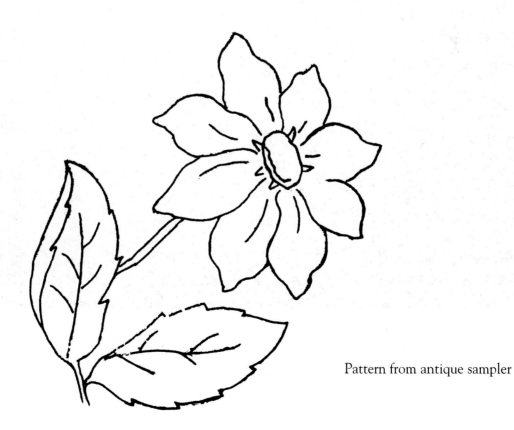

Pattern from antique sampler

ANTIQUE TABLE RUNNER

PREPARATION of FABRIC

When cutting the fabric be generous in the amount you allow for working the piece: the heavy embroidery and washing will reduce the finished size. The edges of the fabric will fray during working so Overlock or machine zig-zag it. Then soak in cold water overnight, rinse, dry and iron. This will remove some of the fabric dressing. If you do not have access to a sewing machine, fold masking tape over the raw edge after ironing. Do not pull the masking tape off, the soaking of the finished work will remove it.

Redrawn from Pim patterns

ANTIQUE THREADS

STARTING and FINISHING of THREADS

If you have already stitched within 1.5cm or so of where you want to start a new section, weave the new thread through these stitches.

When no previous stitching is available an away knot is used – this is the only time in embroidery when a knot is used: tie a knot on the end of your thread and insert the needle from above into the fabric at least 10cm away from the starting point (this will leave the knot on the surface of the fabric). This will give you sufficient thread when you cut the knot off to weave the thread in when the stitching is completed.

When starting a new thread during stitching, note from which point in the stitch the new thread is to emerge BEFORE you take the old thread through to the back of the fabric. Make sure the new thread comes up at that point.

To finish off a thread, weave it in on the back of the work following the track of the existing embroidery. Cut all threads flush on the back, as the back of the embroidery should be as neat as the front.

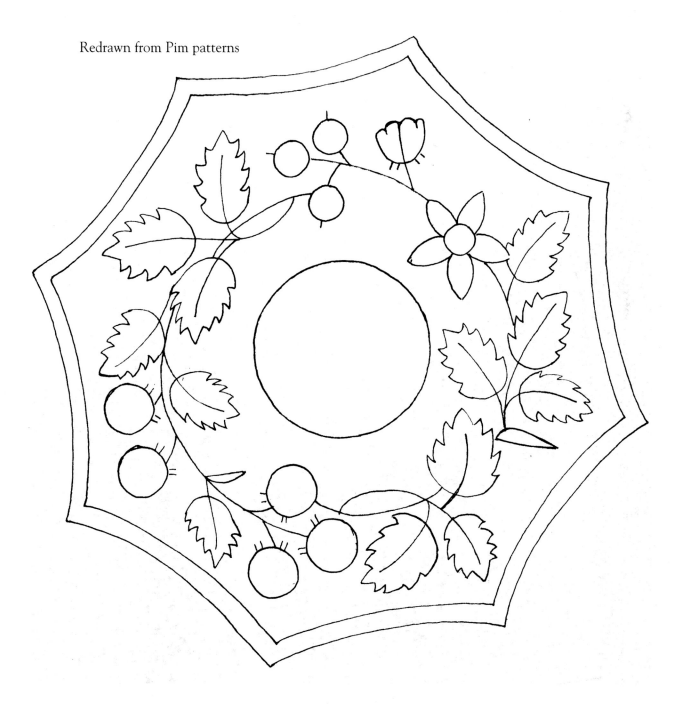

Redrawn from Pim patterns

TABLE RUNNER

TIPS

1. LEAVES

Finish a leaf or petal before stopping work as the tension of the stitch may not be exactly the same when you return to the work. Leaves are usually in sets of an odd number with each leaf in the set being worked the same. The next set is worked differently, try to have a lightly embroidered set next to a heavily worked set. Sometimes a single leaf in a set *is* worked differently symbolising that only God makes things perfect. Do this only once in the entire piece. Leaves do not follow nature except in outline. They can have different stitches on each half of the leaf. Start leaves at the base unless the stitch instructions say otherwise.[15]

2. LEAF POINT

In some cases a tip must be put on a leaf before working the stitch. See S.S. in Glossary.

3. STEMS

These are worked after all attachments, e.g. leaves and flowers, are worked.

4. CHANGING DIRECTION

When changing direction e.g. going around the top of a leaf, turn the fabric and continue as before, do not try to put a stitch on the tip of the leaf.

5. BULLION KNOTS

If making a series of Bullion Knots of the same size make a note of the number of wraps being used by writing it on some masking tape placed on the fabric.

6. FRENCH KNOTS & BULLIONS

Can be made larger or smaller depending on the thickness of the thread and the needle, or by adding more twists.

7. BUTTONHOLE EDGING

It is easier to work the Buttonhole edging if the corners are very slightly rounded. Work your edging before trimming the excess fabric. See Fringe section.

8. WHIPPING

Make sure you have enough thread to complete the full length of the row when Whipping, a new thread can't be introduced satisfactorily during Whipping.

9. PADDING

Padding can be done by laying down straight stitches in the opposite direction to the final stitch and within the design line. Chain Stitch can also be used for padding. For even greater height Chain Stitch can be placed on top of darning.[14]

10. FILLER STITCHES

Filler stitches are used to fill the centre of a flower or leaf and are best worked before the outline stitch.

11. PULLING THROUGH

When pulling through, bring the needle through and then pull the remaining thread by hand – this will give you better control on the tension. Always pull in the direction from which the needle is coming, for example if the needle is coming from right to left, pull to the left.

CUSHION COVER

12. POOR STITCHING

If something you have finished is not to your liking, DO NOT RIP IT OUT, continue on to the next element and, seeing the previous mistake beside you, you will have a better chance of getting it right the next time. Then you can remove the offending stitching. If the type of stitch used on a set of leaves for example does not please, change it by adding to it with whipping or even another stitch on top. This is the case in many of the antique pieces where we have difficulty working out what the stitch is. LET YOUR IMAGINATION FLOW.

13. WORKING DIAGONALLY

Draw a few diagonal lines on the area to be covered or on top of the padding to help keep the direction correct.

14. ADJUSTING THE THREAD

When the length of the thread in the needle needs to be adjusted, place your thumb on the last stitch and then adjust – a stitch can be distorted if tension is put on it.

15. INSTRUCTIONS

Read instructions as far as the comma or the full stop before working the stitch. T.U.L.T., that is, holding the thread under the left thumb, is not required for all stitches so be careful when reading the instructions. Always refer to the diagram at the foot of the instructions and the sampler photograph.

16. DESIGN LINE

You do not have to follow the design line [as it is not permanent]. If the stitches fit better off the line, so be it.

17. STITCH DIRECTORY

It is a good idea to compile your own reference 'directory' of all the different stitches which can be used in Mountmellick Work. This can be done by following the examples in the stitch directory, working the stitches in 4ply coloured cotton so they are clearly visible.

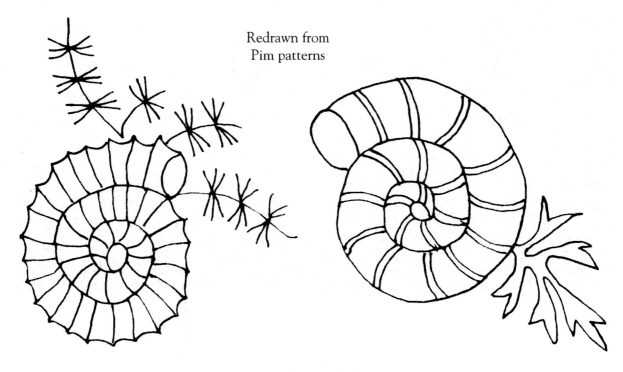

Redrawn from
Pim patterns

27

Redrawn from
Pim patterns

Stitch Directory

Redrawn from
Pim patterns

STITCH INDEX

Note: Mountmellick Work has its own names for some of the stitches and these may differ from other embroidery books. Some stitches also have several different names. Those listed above are the most commonly used.

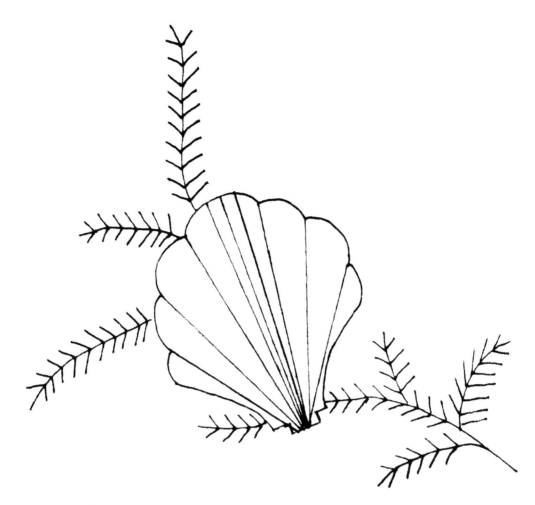

CUSHION COVER

GLOSSARY

Work from left to right (horizontal line) = Work on the design line from left to right.

Work from right to left (horizontal line) = Work on the design line from right to left.

Work from top to bottom (vertical line) = Work on the design line towards yourself.

Work from bottom to top (vertical line) = Work on the design line away from yourself.

R>L = Right to Left
L>R = Left to Right
A>B = Work from point A to point B

P.T. = Pull Through

T.U.L.T. = Hold the base of the working Thread Under the Left Thumb, with the length of the thread lying towards you, i.e. between your thumb and you.

S.T.L. = (Swing the Thread to the Left.) To work the left hand side of a stitch where the thread is to be held under the left thumb: swing the working thread to the left and rotate the needle to have the point facing towards yourself. T.U.L.T. Then insert the needle and pull the thread through over the thread under the thumb.

S.S. = (Straight Stitch.) A Straight Stitch is inserted at the top of a leaf to fill the vacant space which some stitches will leave at the tip of a leaf, e.g. Feather Stitch. It should be done before the main stitch. Bring the thread through on the centre line a short distance from the tip of the leaf and insert it into the tip, pull through. Now continue the stitch as directed.

W.H. = (Whipping.) Work from right to left using the tapestry needle. The needle and thread is brought to the front of the fabric at the base of the first stitch. Insert the needle from above under the second stitch without entering the fabric, pull through. Continue across the row whipping into each stitch. Take the thread through to the back of the fabric at the end of the row, at the base of the last stitch.

*1. = Work this filler stitch before doing the outline. See Tips (Filler Stitches).

STOP, TENSION = Tighten the stitch or the thread around the needle by pulling on the working thread before pulling through.

N.U.T. = (Not Under Thumb.) The thread is not held under the left thumb.

M.M. = Mountmellick.

W.F.T. = (Work from Tip.) To work this stitch on e.g. a leaf, work from the tip to the bottom down the right side and then from the tip down the left side.

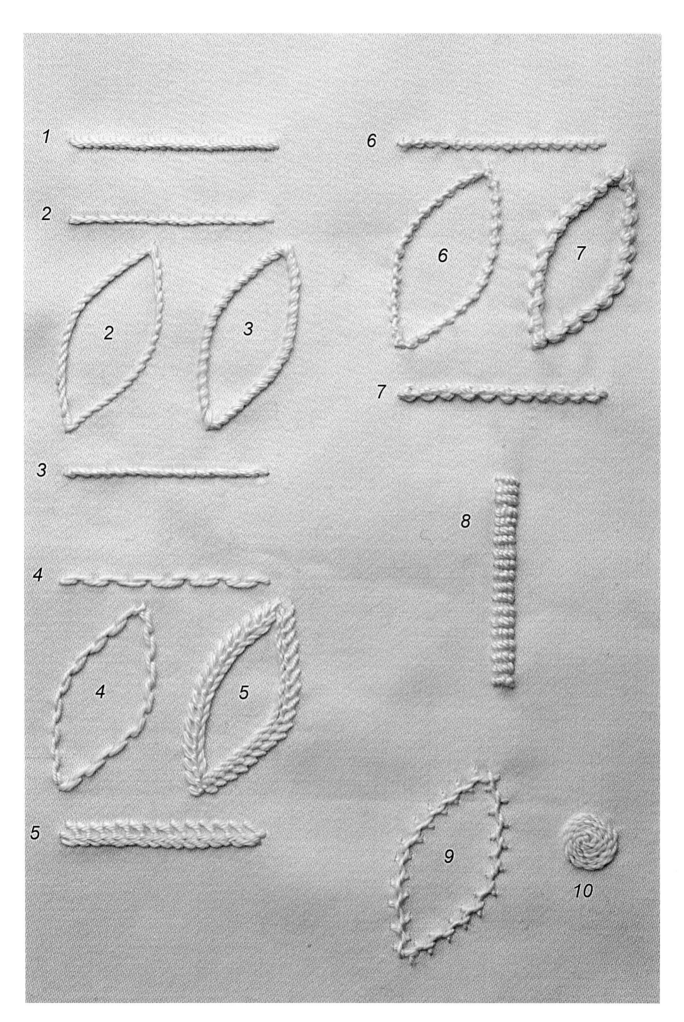

1. STEM STITCH

2. STEM MOUNTMELLICK

6. DOUBLE KNOT STITCH

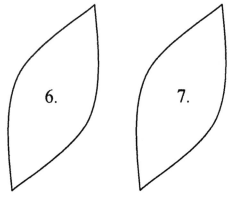

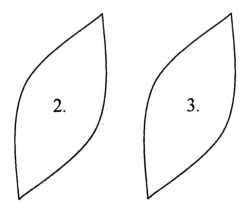

7. DOUBLE THREAD
DOUBLE KNOT STITCH

3. STEM STITCH WHIPPED

4. CABLE STITCH

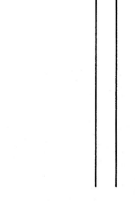

8. STEM STITCH BAND REVERSED

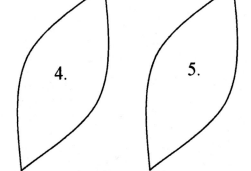

5. STEM with SPACED CORDING

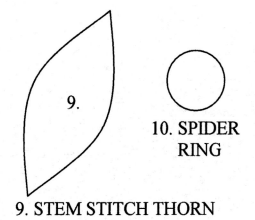

10. SPIDER RING

9. STEM STITCH THORN

I. STEM STITCH = CREWEL STITCH or OUTLINE STITCH[1], also RAILWAY STITCH

Work from left to right of a design line. The thread always emerges on the right side of the previous stitch.

1. Bring the thread up on the line at A.
2. T.U.L.T. Insert the needle below the line at B and in a slanting direction from R>L bring it out at C on the design line. P.T. towards the right.
3. Repeat from 2 bringing the needle out each time close to the previous stitch.

2. STEM STITCH MOUNTMELLICK[6]

Work from left to right on the design line. The thread always emerges on the right side of the previous stitch.
1. Bring the thread up on the line at A.
2. T.U.L.T. Insert the needle a little to the right on the line at B and bring the needle out to the left where the thread emerged at A.
3. P.T. towards the right.
4. Repeat from 2 bringing the needle out each time close to the previous stitch.

3. STEM STITCH WHIPPED[9]

1. Commence with a row of Stem Stitch on the design line.
2. W.H.: working from R>L whip over the stem stitches by passing downwards under each stitch in turn. **DO NOT ENTER THE FABRIC**.
3. At the end of the row take the thread through to the back of the work and fasten off.

4. CABLE STITCH[9]

Work from left to right on a design line.
1. Bring the thread up on the line at A.
2. T.U.L.T. Insert the needle a little to the right on the line at B and bring it back out to the left at C, midway between the insert point A and B. Now P.T.
3. Work the next stitch in the same way but holding down the thread above the row of stitches.
4. Continue in this way alternating the position of the thread with each stitch.

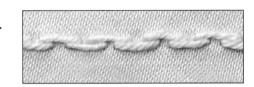

A̶C̶B̶

5. STEM with SPACED CORDING[9]

1. Work a row of spaced Cording Stitch (no. 67, pg 66) from top to bottom of the design lines.
2. Return up the left side of the cording with Stem Stitch (no. 1, pg 36). W.F.T.
* SEE GLOSSARY

6. & 7. DOUBLE KNOT STITCH[9]

Work from top to bottom of a design line.
1. Bring the thread up on the line at A.
2. N.U.T. Slightly lower down take a small slanting stitch from B>C. Now P.T.
3. Pass the needle from R>L under the small stitch you just made. DO NOT ENTER THE FABRIC. STOP. Do not pull all the thread through, leave a small loop.
4. T.U.L.T. and, keeping the loop above the work, pass the needle again from R>L into the same stitch below the loop. DO NOT ENTER FABRIC. STOP. Leave the needle in this position.
5. Tension the thread under the thumb, and then P.T. to form the knot.
6. Repeat from 2. This stitch can also be worked with a double thread.

37

8. STEM STITCH BAND REVERSED

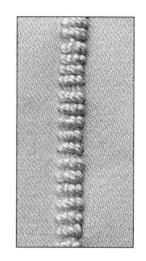

This stitch is used to imitate a book hinge binding as on a needle case. Draw two parallel lines and place work on an embroidery ring. Work from top to bottom and right to left.

1. Working top to bottom single straight stitches are worked between the lines across at right angles and regularly spaced apart.
2. Rotate the fabric so you are now working along the length of the hinge. Commencing at the bottom line and working from R>L the needle proceeds to make a row of whipping stitches under the transverse threads. Passing twice under each thread. DO NOT ENTER THE FABRIC.
3. At the end of the row take the thread through to the back, and weave it along the back straight stitches to the beginning of the row. Bring the thread through to the front again and work a second row as before.
4. Continue to pack in the rows to form the band.

9. STEM STITCH THORN[9]

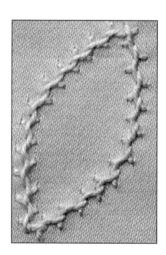

Work from left to right of a design line.
1. Bring the thread up on the line at A.
2. Hold the thread below the line, T.U.L.T. Insert the needle a short distance along the line and bring the point out diagonally to the left below the line, over the thread held by the thumb, B>C. Now P.T. upwards.
3. T.U.L.T. above the line.
4. Insert the needle a short distance further along the line and bring the point out diagonally to the left above the line over the held down thread D>E. P.T. toward yourself.
5. Repeat from 2.

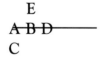

E
A B D
C

10. SPIDER RING[10]

Begin in the centre of the ring, work Stem Stitch (no. 1, pg 36) round and round to the size required. Start with small stitches and these can increase slightly as you progress.

Redrawn from Pim patterns

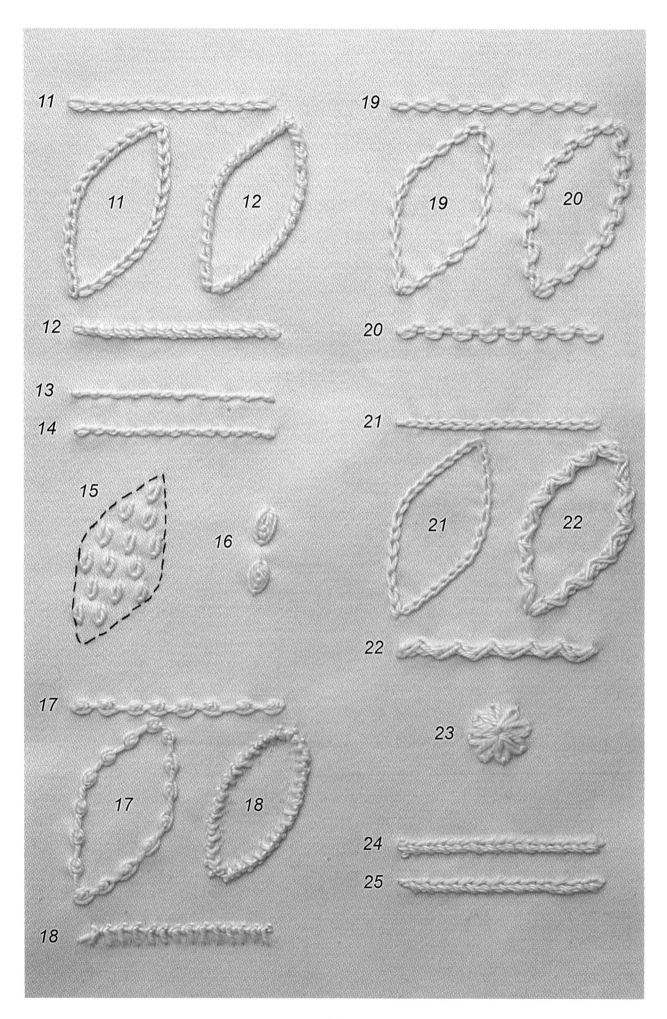

11. CHAIN STITCH

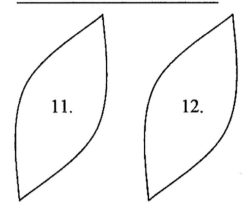

11. 12.

12. CHAIN STITCH WHIPPED

19. CHAIN STITCH LINKED

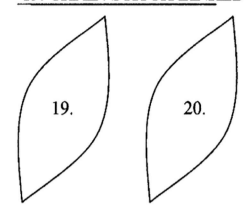

19. 20.

20. DOUBLE CABLE STITCH

13. SNAIL TRAIL

14. SNAIL TRAIL PACKED

21. CHAIN STITCH BROAD

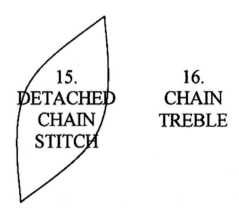

15.
DETACHED
CHAIN
STITCH

16.
CHAIN
TREBLE

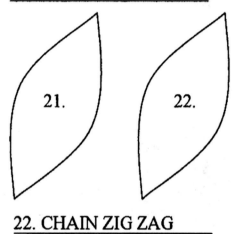

21. 22.

22. CHAIN ZIG ZAG

17. KNOTTED CABLE STITCH

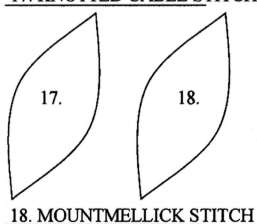

17. 18.

23. LOOP STITCH RING

24. CHAIN DOUBLE ROW

25. CHAIN SINGLE ROW WHIPPED

18. MOUNTMELLICK STITCH

11. CHAIN STITCH[1]

Work from top to bottom on a design line.
1. Bring the thread up at the top of the line.
2. T.U.L.T. Insert the needle where the thread first emerged and bring the point out a short distance along the line. P.T. keeping the working thread under the needle point.
3. Repeat from 2, but now inserting the needle back into the loop of the previous chain.

12. CHAIN STITCH WHIPPED[9]

1. Commence with a row of chain stitch.
2. W.H. Working from right to left whip by passing the thread downwards under each stitch in turn. DO NOT ENTER THE FABRIC.
3. At the end of the row take the thread through to the back of the work and fasten off.
* SEE GLOSSARY.

13. SNAIL TRAIL[1]

Work from top to bottom on a design line. The stitch will appear as a small knot with a straight stitch between each knot.
1. Bring the thread up on the line at A.
2. T.U.L.T. Insert the needle just to the left of the thread on the line again at A. Pick up a very small amount of fabric coming out below on the right hand side of the thread on the line at B. The point of the needle must pass over the thread. P.T.
3 Repeat from 2. a short distance below.

A
B

14. SNAIL TRAIL PACKED = CORAL (A)[8]

Work as for Snail Trail but placing the stitches close together. This stitch gives a firm rope effect.

15. CHAIN STITCH DETACHED[1] = LOOP STITCH *1

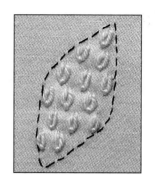

Work in the same way as Chain (no. 11, pg 42) but fasten each loop at the base by taking the thread through to the back outside the loop. This stitch can be used as a filler, in which case it is called Powering. It can also be used as an outline stitch.

16. CHAIN STITCH DOUBLE or TREBLE[10]

To work a small daisy type flower, work a small detached chain stitch in the centre of the petal. Follow this with another detached chain around the first chain. A third stitch could also be applied.

17. KNOTTED CABLE STITCH[9]

Work from top to bottom on a design line.
1. Bring the thread up at the top of the line at A.
2. T.U.L.T. Insert the needle to the left of the thread on the design line at B, slightly below A. Pick up a small amount of fabric coming up on the right hand side of the thread further down on the line, B>C. P.T.
3. Pass the needle from the right side under the straight stitch above the stitch just made. DO NOT ENTER THE FABRIC. P.T.
4. Make one Chain Stitch round the knot just formed.
5. Repeat from 2 but slightly further down.

18. MOUNTMELLICK STITCH[7]

This stitch has not been seen on an antique piece of work in Ireland but it was used in America in 1904. Another version is described in the Coats stitch instruction books.

Work from top to bottom of a design line.
1. Bring the thread up on the line at A.
2. N.U.T. Insert the needle slightly to the right of the line at B and bring it out opposite, on the left of the line at C.   P.T.
3. T.U.L.T. Pass the needle under the stitch from R>L. DO NOT ENTER THE FABRIC. P.T.
4. Keeping the working thread above the stitch, pass the needle from R>L again under the base of the stitch. DO NOT ENTER THE FABRIC. P.T.
5. T.U.L.T. Pass the needle for the third time under the stitch base from R>L.   P.T. Repeat from 2. but slightly further down.

19. CHAIN STITCH LINKED[1]

Work from top to bottom on a design line.
1. Bring the thread up on the line.
2. T.U.L.T. Pass the needle from R>L under the working thread, raise it and hold it in position with the right index finger. DO NOT ENTER THE FABRIC. Turn the point of the needle and, keeping the thread T.U.L.T., enter the fabric on the line and out below also on the line. STOP. TENSION. Make sure the needle passes over the thread under the thumb. P.T.
3. Repeat from 2 keeping the stitches only slightly apart.

20. DOUBLE CABLE STITCH[1] = PERSIAN CORD[8]

This stitch is worked as Chain Stitch Linked but the stitches are placed on alternate sides of the design line. No space is left between the stitches

21. CHAIN STITCH BROAD[9]

Work from top to bottom on a design line. Work this stitch N.U.T.

1. Bring the thread up at the top of the line at A.
2. Make a short straight stitch on the line to B, bringing the needle out further along the line the required length of the chain stitch at C.   P.T.
3. Pass the needle under the straight stitch (A>B) from the right side. DO NOT ENTER THE FABRIC. P.T.
4. Insert the needle into the fabric at the spot where it last emerged, C, bringing it out again further down the line at D ready for the second stitch. P.T.
5. The following stitches you pass the needle under the chain stitch above.

22. CHAIN STITCH ZIG-ZAG[9]

Work from top to bottom of a design line. The needle enters the fabric on the outside edge of each chain at 2., thus placing a second row of Chain Stitch on top of the first row.

1. Work a row of Chain Stitch.
2. Rotate the fabric to continue to stitch back to the start of the row working again from top to bottom.
3. Bring the thread up at the top left of the last chain at A.   P.T.
4. Working in Chain Stitch place each stitch at an angle over the underlying chain, A>B.
5. The next stitch is worked from B>C.
6. Continue along the row to the last chain to produce a zig zag line.

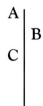

23. LOOP STITCH RING[1]

1. This is a circle of detached chain stitches.
2. Bring the thread up where the centre of the ring is to be, work a detached chain stitch to where the outer edge will be.
3. Continue around the circle bringing the needle up at the same point in the centre each times.

24. CHAIN DOUBLE ROW[11]

This stitch produces a raised row of Chain Stitch. Work from top to bottom and from right to left on a design line.

1. Work a row of Chain Stitch. Bring the thread through to the back of the work.
2. TURN THE FABRIC. Bring the thread up below the last stitch on the right hand side of the row..
3. Working from R>L, W.H. the lower loop of the chain only from inside to outside. DO NOT ENTER THE FABRIC. Continue to the end of the row and bring the thread through to the back of the fabric.
4. TURN THE FABRIC so you now work on the other side of the chain again from right to left. Bring the thread up just below the first chain. W.H. through these loops but this time from outside to inside. DO NOT ENTER THE FABRIC. Bring the thread through to the back of the fabric and fasten off.

25. CHAIN SINGLE ROW WHIPPED[9]

Work from top to bottom and from right to left on a design line.

1. Work a row of Chain Stitch.
2. Work steps 2 and 3 of Chain Double Row.

Redrawn from Pim patterns

47

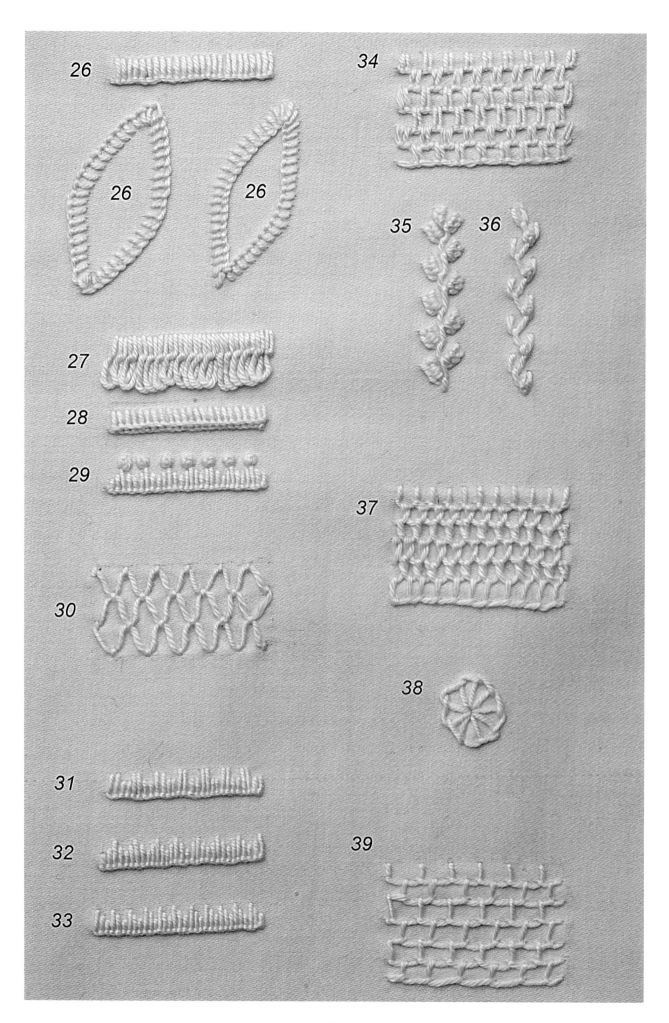

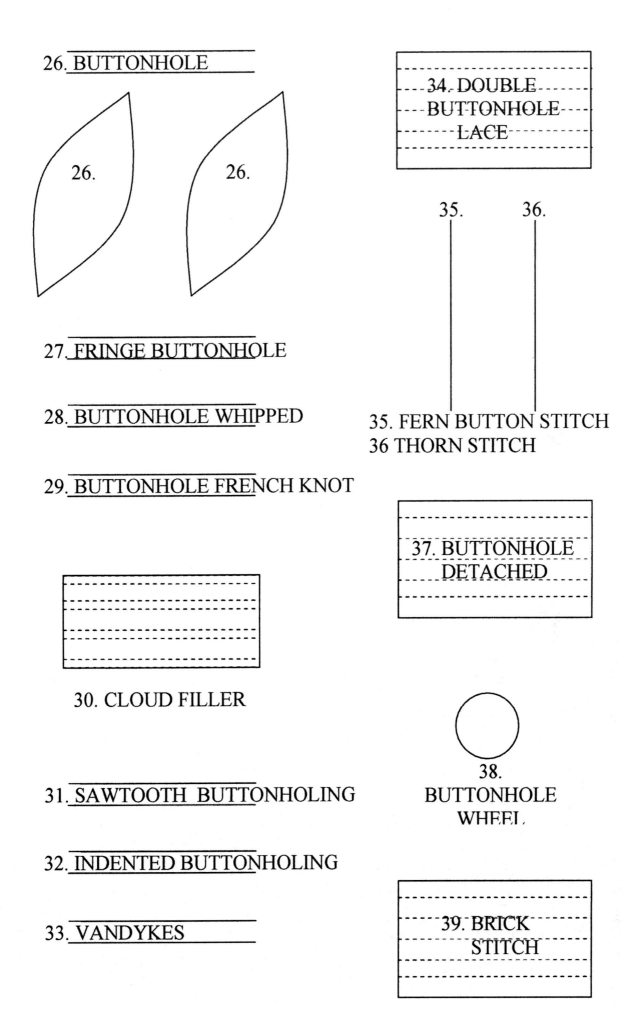

26. BUTTONHOLE

26.   26.

27. FRINGE BUTTONHOLE

28. BUTTONHOLE WHIPPED

29. BUTTONHOLE FRENCH KNOT

30. CLOUD FILLER

31. SAWTOOTH BUTTONHOLING

32. INDENTED BUTTONHOLING

33. VANDYKES

34. DOUBLE BUTTONHOLE LACE

35.   36.

35. FERN BUTTON STITCH
36 THORN STITCH

37. BUTTONHOLE DETACHED

38. BUTTONHOLE WHEEL

39. BRICK STITCH

26. BUTTONHOLE STITCH[1]

This stitch is also used as the hem in Mountmellick Work and when used as such should have a padding of running stitches or a row of Chain Stitch to support it. The stitches are always well packed together. It also forms the base for a fringe. Work from left to right, or right to left with S.T.L. Work on parallel design lines. At other times the stitch can be spaced.
1. Bring the thread up on the lower line at A.
2. T.U.L.T. Insert the needle on the top line at B and out directly below on the bottom line at A. P.T. making sure the needle passes over the held down thread.
3. Repeat from 2.
4. When changing threads finish a stitch by taking the thread through to the back outside the last stitch. Start the new thread by bringing it up on the line inside the last stitch. Also when a round has been completed finish by taking the needle into the base of the first stitch.

27. FRINGE BUTTONHOLE[1]

Work from left to right on parallel design lines. This stitch is used as a finishing edge when the knitted fringe is not used. The stitches are packed closely together.
1. Bring the thread up on the line.
2. T.U.L.T. Work one Buttonhole Stitch, any of the variations can be used.
3. The second stitch is also a buttonhole stitch but it is not pulled through fully. Leave a loop approximately 1cm long.
4. Hold both the loop and the T.U.L.T. Work an ordinary Buttonhole Stitch. P.T.
5. Again work the fringe buttonhole stitch. Before placing under the thumb check the length of the loop is the same as the previous loop. This can be done by passing the needle tip into the current and the previous loop and pulling the thread downwards to check both lengths, adjust if necessary. DO NOT PULL THROUGH. Withdraw the needle and place the thumb over the loops and the thread. Work an ordinary Buttonhole stitch. P.T.
6. Repeat from 5 checking back through two loops plus the current loop each time.

28. BUTTONHOLE WHIPPED[9]

Work from left to right on parallel design lines.
1. Work a row of Buttonhole stitch slightly spaced apart.
2. Bring the thread up again at the start of the row close to the base of the first stitch.
3. W.H. along the row picking up the upright part of the stitch. DO NOT ENTER THE FABRIC. At the end of the row bring the thread through the fabric to finish off on the back.
4. One or several rows of whipping can be worked, but always start at the beginning of each row for each additional row of whipping.

* SEE GLOSSARY.

29. BUTTONHOLE FRENCH KNOT[1]

Any style of Buttonhole Stitch can be worked and subsequently have a French Knot (no. 64, pg 64) added to the highest point.

30. CLOUD [WAVE] FILLER[9] *[1]

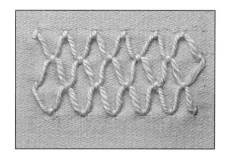

Work from left to right and right to left. Work on parallel design lines drawn across the area to be filled.
1. First work a row of small upright stitches evenly spaced. Then do a second and subsequent row alternating the positions on the stitches to fill the area.
2. Bring the thread up under the upright stitch at the top left hand side of the work.
3. Begin to weave through the stitches and between the rows as shown on the diagram. DO NOT ENTER THE FABRIC.
4. Take the needle through the fabric only at the start and finish of each row.

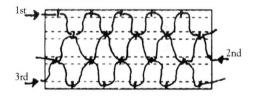

31. SAWTOOTH BUTTONHOLING[1]

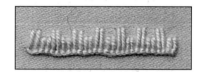

Work from left to right on parallel design lines.
1. Two long stitches are worked followed by two shorter Buttonhole stitches.

32. INDENTED BUTTONHOLING[1]

Work from left to right on parallel design lines.
1. This is a series of graduated lengths of Buttonhole stitches arranged in an upturned V shape. It consists of a 4 stitch arrangement.

33. VANDYKES[8]

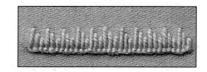

Work from left to right on parallel design lines.
1. This is any series of graduated lengths of Buttonhole stitches arranged to form a triangular shape. It consists of a 3 stitch arrangement.

34. DOUBLE BUTTONHOLE LACE⁹ *I

Work from left to right and right to left on parallel design lines drawn across the area to be covered.

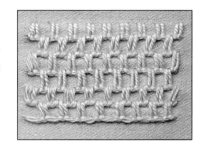

1. Starting at the top, bring the thread up on the left on the first baseline for the first stitch.
2. T.U.L.T. Work two small Buttonhole stitches close together. Leave a space and work another two stitches. Do not have the linking thread between the stitches too tight.
3. Continue across to the end of the row. Bring the thread through to the back of the fabric.
4. Bring the thread up at the base of the second row and now working from right to left. S.T.L. Insert the needle in the space between the previous row of stitches above the linking thread on its design line and out directly below on the second line. Work two Buttonhole stitches.
5. Continue to work the lace forming the pattern.

35. FERN BUTTONHOLE = BUTTON LOOP STITCH⁴

Work from top to bottom and bottom to top. This is a stitch used for ferns.

1. Work a row of Feather Stitch, [no. 40, pg 56] each arm of the feather should be large enough to hold three Buttonhole stitches.
2. Working now from bottom to top bring the thread up at the base of the last Feather Stitch arm.
3. Work three Detached Buttonhole stitches [no. 37, pg 53] on the arm. DO NOT ENTER THE FABRIC. Take the thread through to the back of the fabric at the base of the last stitch.
4. Carry the thread across the back of the fabric to the base of the next Feather Stitch arm on the other side. Repeat from 3.

36. THORN STITCH³

Work from top to bottom of a design line.

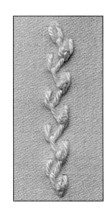

1. Work a single Coral Stitch [no. 42, pg 56] on both sides starting with the left one. S.T.L.
2. T.U.L.T. Pass the point of the needle under the thread, and over and under and over and under the thread again. Keeping the twist on the needle with the right index finger, turn the point of the needle upwards and carry it over the strand which runs across from the first stitch to the second and insert it into the fabric where it last emerged. Bring it out below the strand and over the thread held by the thumb. STOP TENSION. P.T.
3. Repeat from I.

37. BUTTONHOLE DETACHED[9] *I

Work from left to right and then right to left, also top to bottom. Draw lines across the design shape [see pattern, pg 49]. Make small loose stitches. This stitch looks best when worked with a fine thread.

1. Bring the thread up on the first design line on the left side at the top of the shape.
2. Work a row of small Buttonhole stitches spaced along the top from L>R.
3. Now going from R>L and S.T.L. work a row of Detached Buttonhole stitches into each bar of the previous row. S.T.L. DO NOT ENTER THE FABRIC. DO NOT OVER TENSION and leave small loose stitches. At the end of the row take the needle through to the back of the fabric to anchor the row.
4. Bring the thread up on the next design line.
5. Working now from L>R work a row of Detached Buttonhole Stitch into the loops of the previous row as at 3. At the end of the row take the needle through to the back of the fabric.
6. Repeating rows 3–5 not included the last row. Take care not to pull the stitches too tightly as this will spoil the lace effect.
7. The last row is worked through the fabric, this attaching the lace to the fabric.

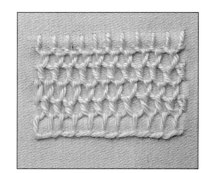

38. BUTTONHOLE WHEEL[9]

1. Bring the thread up on the outside edge of the ring.
2. Work a spaced Buttonhole Stitch taking the needle down in the centre of the ring for every stitch, and bringing it out a little to the right on the outer edge at each stitch. This stitch works well in fine thread on small berries.

39. BRICK STITCH[1] *I

A filler stitch which is worked the same way as Buttonhole Stitch from top to bottom, R>L and L>R. The base part of the stitch is approx. twice as long as the upright part. The second and following rows are worked into the spaces between the above stitches. [See pattern, pg 49].

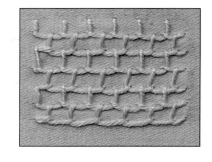

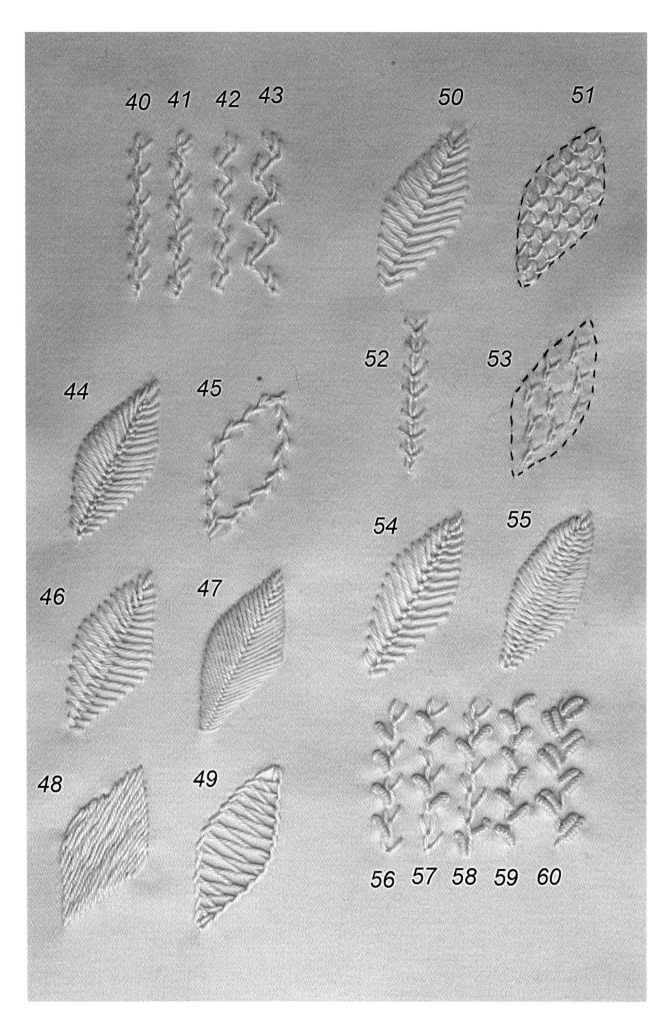

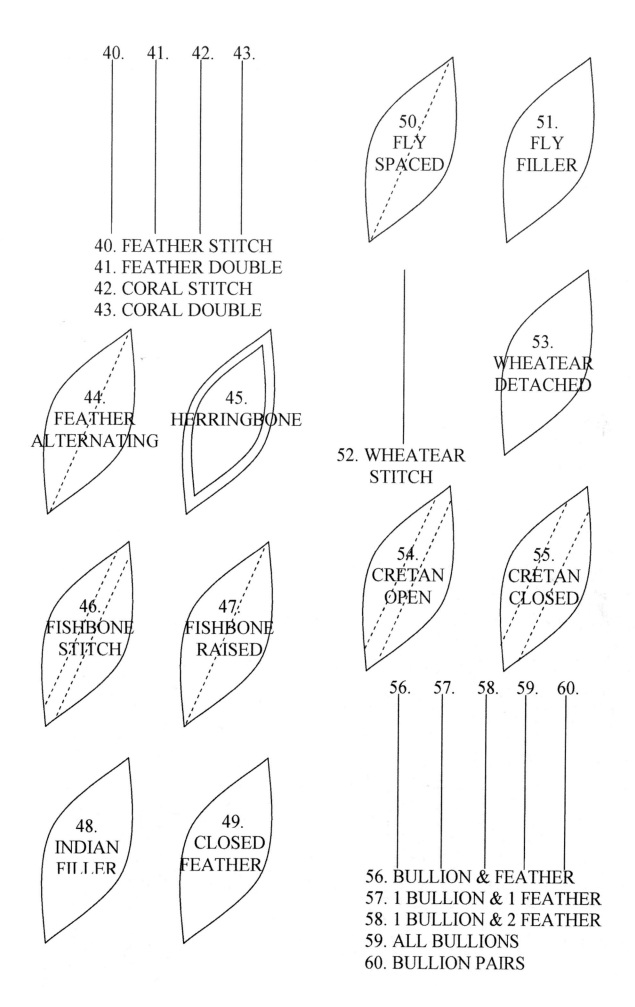

40. FEATHER STITCH
41. FEATHER DOUBLE
42. CORAL STITCH
43. CORAL DOUBLE

50. FLY SPACED

51. FLY FILLER

44. FEATHER ALTERNATING

45. HERRINGBONE

53. WHEATEAR DETACHED

52. WHEATEAR STITCH

46. FISHBONE STITCH

47. FISHBONE RAISED

54. CRETAN OPEN

55. CRETAN CLOSED

48. INDIAN FILLER

49. CLOSED FEATHER

56. BULLION & FEATHER
57. 1 BULLION & 1 FEATHER
58. 1 BULLION & 2 FEATHER
59. ALL BULLIONS
60. BULLION PAIRS

40. FEATHER STITCH[1]

Work from top to bottom of a design line. If working on a leaf draw a perpendicular work line down the leaf centre and work from the leaf edge to the central line. S.S.

1. Bring the thread up at the top of the design line, or on the central line below the S.S. if working on a leaf.
2. T.U.L.T. Insert the needle slightly above to the right of the line and in a slanting direction coming out below on the design line, with the point of the needle passing over the thread held down by the thumb, P.T.
3. S.T.L. Insert the needle slightly above on the left side and in a slanting direction coming out below on the design line, with the point of the needle passing over the thread held down by the thumb, P.T.
4. Repeat from 2 above working down the line and alternating from R>L.

41. FEATHER DOUBLE STITCH[1]

Worked as above, with two stitches placed every time on each side.

42. CORAL STITCH (B)[1]

Work as for Feather except the arm of the stitch is straight where in Feather it is slanting, so you do not work on the design line. Insert the needle a short distance from the right side of the line and bring it up further down directly below. Do not forget T.U.L.T. Repeat on the left side. S.T.L.

43. CORAL DOUBLE STITCH[1]

Work as above, but with two stitches placed every time on each side.

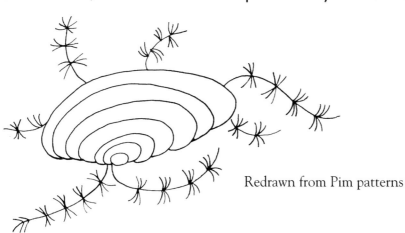

Redrawn from Pim patterns

44. FEATHER ALTERNATING STITCH[9] = CRETAN STITCH

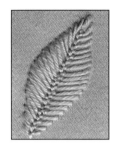

1. Work the same as Feather Stitch (no. 40, pg 56) for a leaf with S.S. To make the design in the centre of the stitch do not bring the needle through on the central line. Instead, when working the right hand stitch bring the needle up just short of this line on its right hand side and vice versa.

45. HERRINGBONE STITCH[1]

Work from left to right using two parallel design lines.
1. Bring the thread up on the lower line.
2. T.U.L.T. Insert the needle on the upper line a little to the right, taking a small stitch to the left. P.T.
3. N.U.T. Insert the needle on the lower line a little to the right and take a small stitch to the left with the thread above the needle.
4. These two movements are worked throughout.

46. FISHBONE STITCH[9]

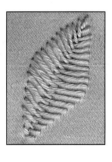

Worked from top to bottom on a leaf, with two parallel lines added down the centre. Worked N.U.T.
1. S.S. Bring the thread up at A. P.T.
2. Insert the needle down with a sloping stitch to the left central line at B and out at C. P.T.
3. Make a similar sloping stitch to overlap the previous stitch at right central line D to E. P.T.
4. Repeat from 2 slightly further down.

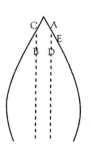

Pattern from Antique Sampler

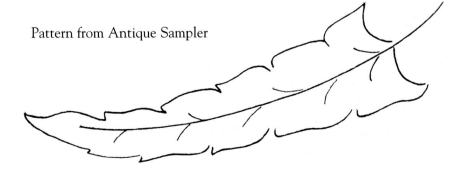

47. FISHBONE STITCH RAISED = LEAF STITCH[8]

Worked from top to bottom on a leaf. This is a self padded stitch.
1. Bring the thread up at A (the tip of the leaf).
2. Insert the needle at B halfway down the centre and bring the needle out at C immediately opposite on the left outer line. P.T.
3. From now on work only the outlines. Insert the needle at D near the top right, and bring it out at E opposite left. P.T.
4. Insert the needle at F right and emerge at G [below C] opposite, on the left outline. P.T.
5. Continue with this D>E and F>G movement, moving down the length of the leaf.
6. The stitches at A and B are only made at the beginning. Repeat from 3.

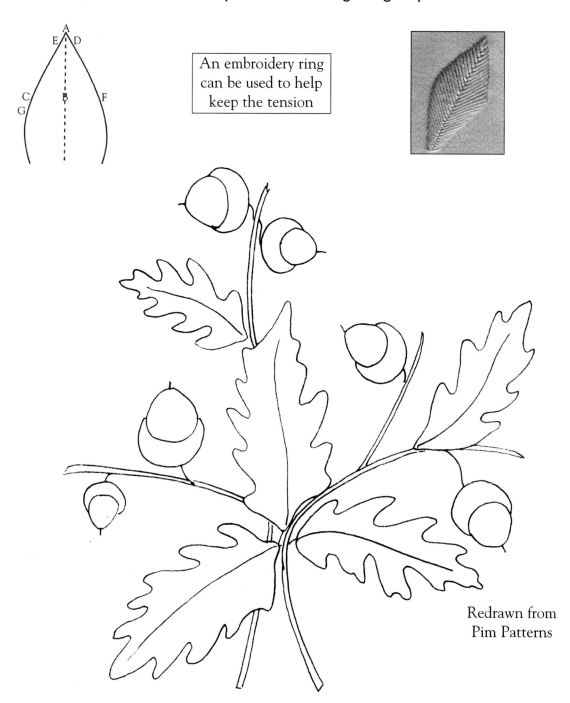

An embroidery ring can be used to help keep the tension

Redrawn from
Pim Patterns

58

48. INDIAN FILLER

This stitch may be used as a substitute for Satin Stitch (no. 61, pg 64) to cover a large area up to 8cm. It is worked best if started at the centre of the baseline, and worked to the right, followed by working from the centre to the left. Work from the bottom of the space to be filled to the top. The second part of the stitch is from the top to the bottom. Use an embroidery ring to control the tension. The tie down stitches must be randomly placed, not too small and should blend into the base stitch. Think Satin Stitch as you work.

1. Bring the thread up on the line at the bottom of the area to be filled at A.
2. Insert the needle into the top line of the area to form a long straight stitch at B. P.T.
3. Now working downwards place the 'tie' over the stitch just made as follows (there can be one, two or even three ties to cover the base stitch depending on its length). Bring the point of the needle through under the base stitch just below at C. P.T.
4. Insert the needle further down on the right side of the base thread at D. P.T.
5. Repeat steps 3 and 4, e.g from E>F, leaving a space between the tie stitches.
6. Repeat from 1, keeping the base stitches close together and staggering the tie stitches.

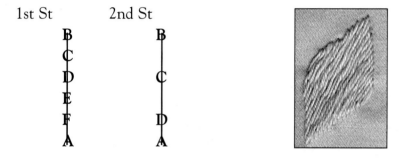

59

49. CLOSED FEATHER STITCH

This stitch is best suited to a narrow leaf; it is worked the same way as Feather Stitch (no. 40, pg 56) on a leaf without using a central line. The needle is placed only on the outline of the design, for example on the right side of the design insert the needle in and out on the right line, and on the left S.T.L. insert the needle in and out on the left line. When inserting the needle it must go just above the base thread of the previous stitch on that side.

50. FLY STITCH SPACED[11]

This is a single stitch, not attached to the following one. Work from top to bottom on a leaf, can also be worked packed. Add a central line. S.S.
1. Bring the thread up at the left, A.
2. T.U.L.T. Insert the needle to the right on the same level, B.
3. Bring the needle out on the centre line at C. keeping the needle point above the thread held down by the left thumb. P.T.
4. Insert the needle immediately below the stitch at D. P.T.
5. Repeat from 1.

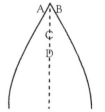

51. FLY STITCH FILLER[9] *1

Start at the tip of the leaf and work a single small Fly Stitch [no. 50, pg 60] in the ordinary way. In the subsequent rows, these small fly stitches are placed in the space between the above stitches. Work a half stitch where necessary on the outside edge. The rows are repeated thus, touching each other, to form the filler. Can also be used as a single stitch for filling as with Chain Stitch Detached [See no. 15, pg 43].

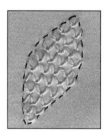

52. WHEAT-EAR STITCH[1]

Work from top to bottom of a design line N.U.T.
1. Bring the thread up on the line at A.
2. Work a straight stitch to B. and across the back to C. P.T.
3. Insert the needle at the point where it first emerged. A. bring the thread out at D. P.T.
4. Pass the needle under the two straight stitches above. DO NOT ENTER THE FABRIC. P.T.
5. Insert the needle at D. again and bring it out a little further down at E. P.T.
6. Repeat from 2.

53. WHEAT-EAR DETACHED⁹ *1

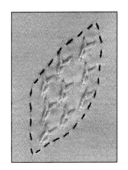

1. Follow steps 1–4 for Wheat-ear Stitch (no. 52, pg 60).
2. Re-insert the needle at D to complete the stitch.

54. CRETAN STITCH OPEN⁹

Work from top to bottom on a leaf. Add two parallel lines. This stitch changes in appearance depending on how far apart these parallel lines are placed. The stitch method is the same as for no. 44 except you work on two central lines.

1. S.S. Bring the thread up near the tip on the leaf, on the left hand outside edge at A.
2. T.U.L.T. and insert the needle on the right hand outside edge at B and bring it up slightly further down on the line at C. P.T.
3. S.T.L. To work the left side of the leaf, insert the needle at D on the outside edge and up to the centre left line at E. P.T., keeping the thread under the point of the needle.
4. Repeat steps 2 and 3.

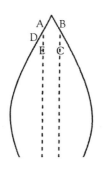

55. CRETAN STITCH CLOSED

For a solid leaf work exactly as described for Cretan Stitch Open, but place the stitches closer together.

56 – 60 BULLION WITH FEATHER¹

Work from the top of the design line.
56. One side is worked in Bullion Knot and the other in Feather Stitch.
57. A Bullion and a Feather Stitch are worked alternately on each side.
58. One Bullion is worked followed by two Feather stitches on each side.
59. Bullions are worked throughout in Feather style.
60. Bullions worked in pairs throughout in Feather style.

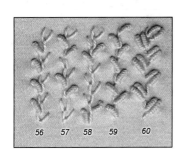

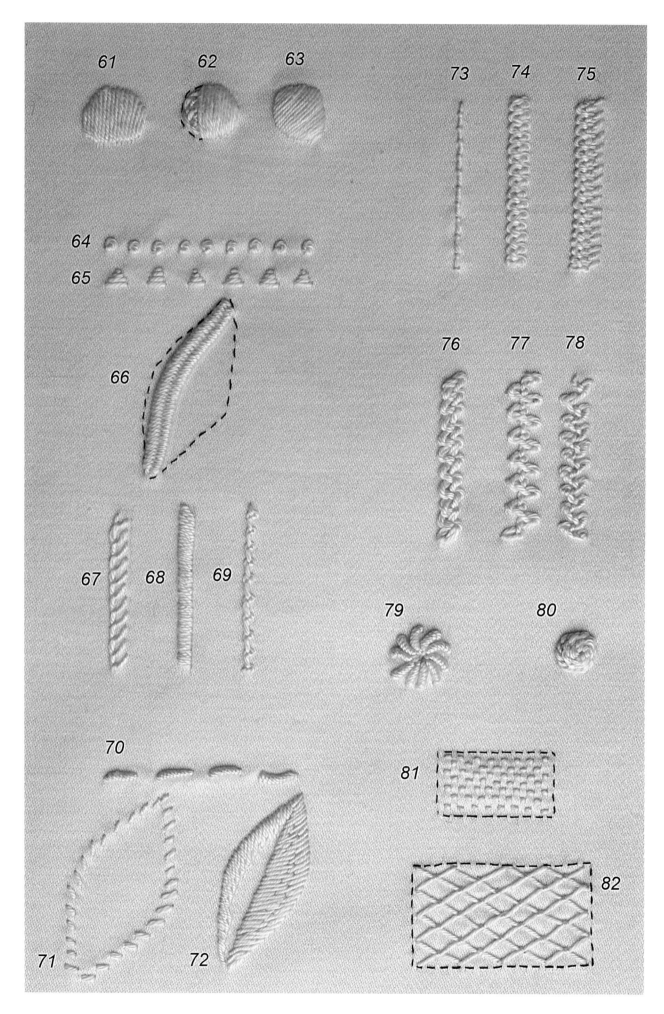

61 62 63

73 74 75

64
65

76 77 78

66

79 80

67 68 69

70

81

71 72

82

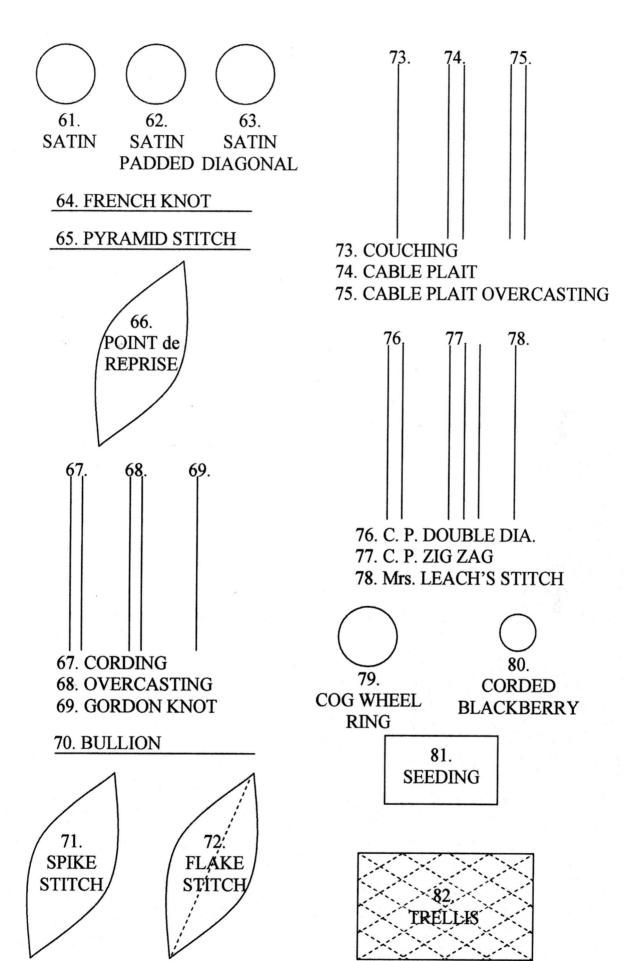

61.
SATIN

62.
SATIN
PADDED

63.
SATIN
DIAGONAL

64. FRENCH KNOT

65. PYRAMID STITCH

66.
POINT de
REPRISE

67. 68. 69.

67. CORDING
68. OVERCASTING
69. GORDON KNOT

70. BULLION

71.
SPIKE
STITCH

72.
FLAKE
STITCH

73. 74. 75.

73. COUCHING
74. CABLE PLAIT
75. CABLE PLAIT OVERCASTING

76. 77. 78.

76. C. P. DOUBLE DIA.
77. C. P. ZIG ZAG
78. Mrs. LEACH'S STITCH

79.
COG WHEEL
RING

80.
CORDED
BLACKBERRY

81.
SEEDING

82.
TRELLIS

61. SATIN STITCH[1]

This stitch is worked from bottom to top of the design line. If the stitch length is greater than approx. 2cm use Indian Filler instead. Work the Satin Stitch from the centre of the baseline to the right and then from the centre to the left across the required area. [See More Tips; Working Roses.] Using an embroidery ring and working the stitch in two separate movements will give greater control of the tension.

1. Bring the thread up on the bottom line at A. P.T.
2. Insert the needle at B. P.T.
3. Repeat 1. and 2. placing the stitches close together to fill the space.

62. SATIN STITCH PADDED

Work rows of Chain (no. 11, pg 42) or Straight Stitch in the design area to be covered, in the opposite direction to which the Satin Stitch will be worked; a thicker thread can be used. Work the Satin Stitch as above.

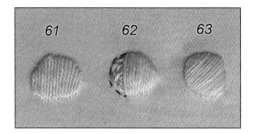

63. SATIN STITCH DIAGONAL

The stitch can also be worked diagonally with or without padding following the instructions for Satin Stitch.
* See Tips.

64. FRENCH KNOT[1]

Using an embroidery ring helps to keep a good tension on this knot.
1. Bring the thread up at the required position.
2. T.U.L.T. Encircle the thread twice with the needle, holding the twists on the needle with the right index finger.
3. Still holding the thread under the thumb, turn the needle back down to the starting point and insert it close to where the thread first emerged. STOP. Hold the point of the needle stable at the back of the work with two fingers of the left hand.
4. TENSION the knot still with T.U.L.T. If the knot is in the correct position, P.T. If not at this stage just retract the needle and repeat from 2.
* See Tips.

65. PYRAMID STITCH[3] *I

Draw parallel guidelines across the area to be filled and place the fabric in an embroidery ring. Starting at the base of the pyramid with the longest stitch a series of Satin stitches are worked to form a triangle. This stitch is used as a filler so the pyramids are quite small, e.g. three to five stitches in total.]

66. POINT DE REPRISE[3] *I

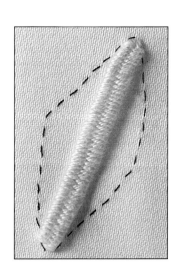

Work from bottom to top of design. Use an embroidery ring.
1. Bring the thread up at the base of the area to be filled and insert the needle at the top of the area. P.T.
2. Work another long straight stitch from the top to the base.
3. Repeat 1 and 2. All four threads should now lie flat side by side on the surface of the fabric.
4. Bring the needle up on the right hand side of the threads at the base A. Change to a small tapestry needle.
5. Pass the needle over the first two threads and under the second two threads coming out at B. P.T. DO NOT ENTER THE FABRIC.
6. Reverse the direction of the needle. Now working from L>R pass it over the two threads you just went under and go under the next two threads. DO NOT ENTER THE FABRIC. P.T.
7. Continue to weave in this manner along the whole length of the laid threads never having entered the fabric.
8. Bring the thread through to the back of the fabric and finish off.

B ‖‖ A

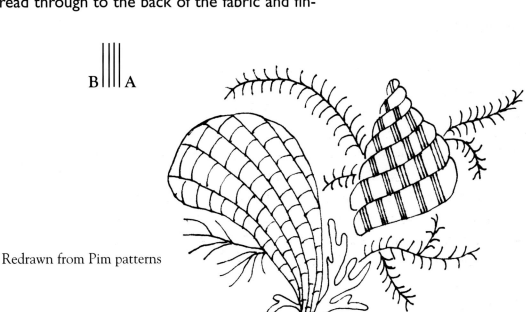

Redrawn from Pim patterns

67. CORDING[1]

Work from top to bottom on two parallel design lines.
1. Bring the thread up at the top of the left line.
2. T.U.L.T. Insert the needle a little lower and on the right line A and bring it out a little lower and slanting to the left line B point of the needle over the thread held down by the thumb. P.T.
3. T.U.L.T. Insert the needle parallel to where the thread comes out on to the right line C. below the previous stitch. Bring the needle out slanting to the left line, D. P.T. over the thread held by the thumb.
4. Repeat 3. The stitches should be placed close together to give the appearance of a cord.

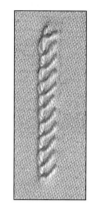

68. OVERCASTING[1]

Work from left to right, or bottom to top, and on two parallel lines. The design area can be padded first or not and the stitches spaced or packed. This is a type of Satin Stitch. Note the thread is N.U.T.
1. Bring the thread up on the bottom line. A.
2. Insert the needle on the top line, B. and bring it up below on the bottom line at C in a direction slanting from R>L. P.T. Repeat across the line.
3. Every stitch is worked in the same way, closely and regularly, side by side. This stitch can be worked to any width.

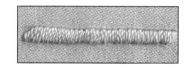

69. GORDON KNOT[3]

Work from left to right of a design line.
1. Bring the thread up on the line at A.
2. T.U.L.T. Lift the thread up with the point of the needle and hold it in place with the right index finger.
3. Rotate the needle so as the point enters the fabric a small distance above the line at B. The point of the needle is facing yourself. Bring the needle up directly below the line at C keeping the thread under the left thumb. STOP.
4. TENSION. Return T.U.L.T. P.T. towards yourself.
5. Repeat from 2, leaving a small space between each knot. There should be a long stitch and a knot on the working line.

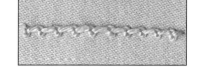

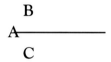

70. BULLION KNOT = WORMS[1]

The size of this stitch depends on the thickness of the needle, the thread and the number of twists used.
1. Bring the thread up at the base of where you want the bullion to be. T.U.L.T.
2. Insert the needle into the fabric just short of the top point of the length of the bullion and up again where the thread first came through. STOP. DO NOT PULL THROUGH.
3. Wrap the thread which is at the point of the needle around the needle point sufficient times to cover the same length as the piece of fabric the needle has picked up.
4. Hold the thread and wraps firmly under the left thumb. P.T.
5. Gently pull the thread upwards so that the wraps turn over and cover the fabric first picked up. TENSION.
6. Insert the needle at the top of the bullion thus tying it down. P.T.

71. SPIKE STITCH[3]

These are long and short stitches placed diagonally on the outside of an already worked leaf. The best effect is achieved if the short stitches are worked towards the base and the top of the leaf, with the longer ones in the centre. See pg 78.

72. FLAKE STITCH[1]

Draw a line down the centre of the leaf, and use the embroidery ring. The stitch can be spaced or packed. Working up the right hand side of the leaf first.

1. Work a diagonal row of long and short stitches starting at the bottom working from the centre to the outside line. The inside edge should be jagged and the outside smooth.
2. The subsequent rows can be worked from top to bottom as well as from bottom to top. Fill in the spaces of a previous row of short stitches with a long stitch and a long stitch with a short stitch. Work only to the central line.
3. Start again now on the left side of the leaf and repeat from row 1.

73. COUCHING[1]

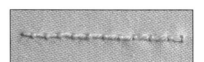

Work from right to left of a design line. Two threads are required for this stitch. A single thread can be couched or for a heavier effect several threads.

1. Bring the thread to be couched up on the design line at the right hand side. This thread most be long enough to run the full length of the line being worked, plus enough to finish off. Now remove the needle.
2. Bring the second thread, which is the working thread, up also on the right hand side and slightly below the line.
3. Hold the thread to be couched T.U.L.T. Take small vertical stitches at regular intervals along the line over the laid thread.
4. At the end of the row take both threads to the back and weave in.

74. CABLE PLAIT[1] = BRAID STITCH[8]

Work from top to bottom and use a short length of thread. If the stitch goes wrong it has to be cut out. This stitch is made between two parallel design lines. Let the stitch sit on the surface of the fabric. Do not pull too tightly or it will gather in the middle of the channel.

1. Bring the thread up in the centre of the channel at A.

2. T.U.L.T. loosely, insert the needle under this thread from below and lift holding the thread on the needle with the right index finger.

3. Continue to T.U.L.T. Rotate the point of the needle downwards to insert it on the right hand line at B and up on the left hand line opposite at C. STOP. [Note: all the threads formed by the lifting thread must lie on the fabric above the needle. The thread under the thumb must be under the point of the needle.]

4. TENSION the thread that is under the thumb, replace T.U.L.T. At this stage the stitch should look like the start of a figure of 8 on its side. P.T. towards the left and return the thread under the left thumb.

5. Repeat from 2. The stitches are packed together.

A second method is to follow the instructions for the Gordon Knot (no. 69, pg 67) but make the stitches wider and pack them together. (This method will not work for the Diagonal Cable Plait.)

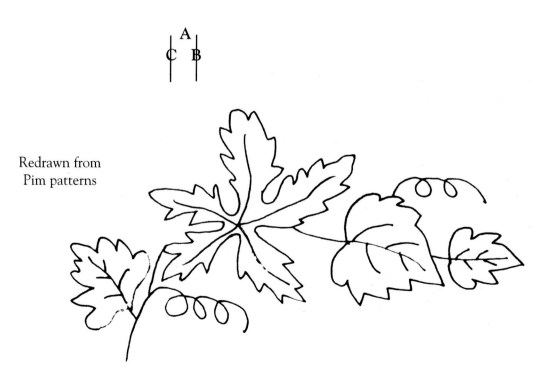

Redrawn from
Pim patterns

69

75. CABLE PLAIT AND OVERCASTING[1]

A small straight stitch is put on the side of each Cable Plait. If
the straight stitch is added only to alternate stitches the effect
is of a thorny stem.

1. Work a row of Cable Plait (no. 74, pg 69).
2. Working from the bottom of the row upwards, add a small
   straight stitch at a slight angle upwards through the right
   hand side loops of the Cable Plaits.

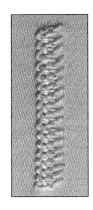

76. CABLE PLAIT DOUBLE DIAGONAL[9]

This stitch is worked with a double thread and the stitch is
placed on the diagonal between the lines. Work from top to
bottom on parallel lines, using the stitch method for No. 74.

1. Bring the thread through at A.
2. Insert the dressed needle at B on the right hand side, and
   out at A again on the left line.
3. TENSION. P.T.
4. The next stitch is inserted at D>C repeating steps 2 and 3.

77. CABLE PLAIT ZIG-ZAG[9]

This stitch is worked on alternate lines. Draw three parallel
lines and place one stitch on the right hand line and the centre line, and then one on the centre line and left hand line.

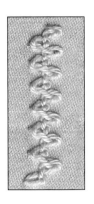

78. MRS LEACH'S STITCH[8]

Work from left to right on a design line stitches are placed close together.

1. Bring the thread up on the line at A.
2. Insert the needle slightly to the right, in on the line at B and up again just above the line at C. The needle should point away from you. DO NOT PULL THROUGH.
3. With your right hand place the thread coming from the left under the eye of the needle, then crossing the needle give the thread two wraps under the point of the needle from right to left. DO NOT WRAP IT TOO TIGHT.
4. Place the left thumb on the needle and the wraps, P.T. TENSION.
5. The next stitch and every alternate stitch is done exactly the reverse way, that is having the needle pointing towards yourself, when it is on the line D coming up at E.

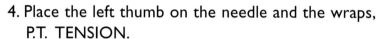

79. COG WHEEL RING[1]
This ring consists of Bullion stitches (no. 70, pg 67) worked in a circle.

Pattern from antique piece

80. CORDED BLACKBERRY[9]

This is a couched cord, stitched in a circle to make a blackberry.

1. Attach a thread to the fabric at the centre of the blackberry with two small stitches. THIS MUST BE DONE FIRST so as to have the design ready to receive the cord.
2. To make the cord use a 12inch length of thread. Pass the thread through a safety pin which is pinned to the arm of a chair or your trousers (not your skirt). Make sure the thread lies on the open bar of the pin. Draw the two ends together and twist them until the forming cord starts to bend.
3. Pull the cord straight and continue to hold the end in the left hand while pinching the cord halfway down its length with the right hand. Bring the left hand down to the safety pin until you are gripping both ends of the cord with the left hand.
4. Release the pinch and the cord will twist on itself. If necessary smooth out any wrinkles in the cord. Open the safety pin and, continuing to hold both ends of the cord in the left hand, attach these open ends with a few stitches to the centre of the design,
5. With a stabbing stitch attach the rest of the cord to the design, placing the cord in a circle to fill the space.
6. Do another round on top of the last round and continue inwards to the centre.
7. Pass the needle through the loop at the end of the cord, insert the needle down through the centre of the blackberry and pull the end of the cord down into the centre. Weave the thread at the back of the work.

81. SEEDING[6] *1

Tiny straight stitches are placed over the area to be filled. They can be set in a pattern or scattered. The use of an embroidery ring helps to keep the tension correct.

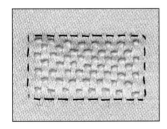

82. TRELLIS[2] *1

1. Draw guidelines as on pg 63.
2. Using a embroidery ring lay down rows of straight stitches right across the space in one direction.
3. Lay a second row of threads across in the opposite direction.
4. Place a small stitch to hold down the threads where they cross at each intersection. This can also be worked in Chain Stitch.

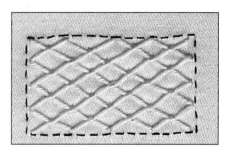

Redrawn from Pim patterns

73

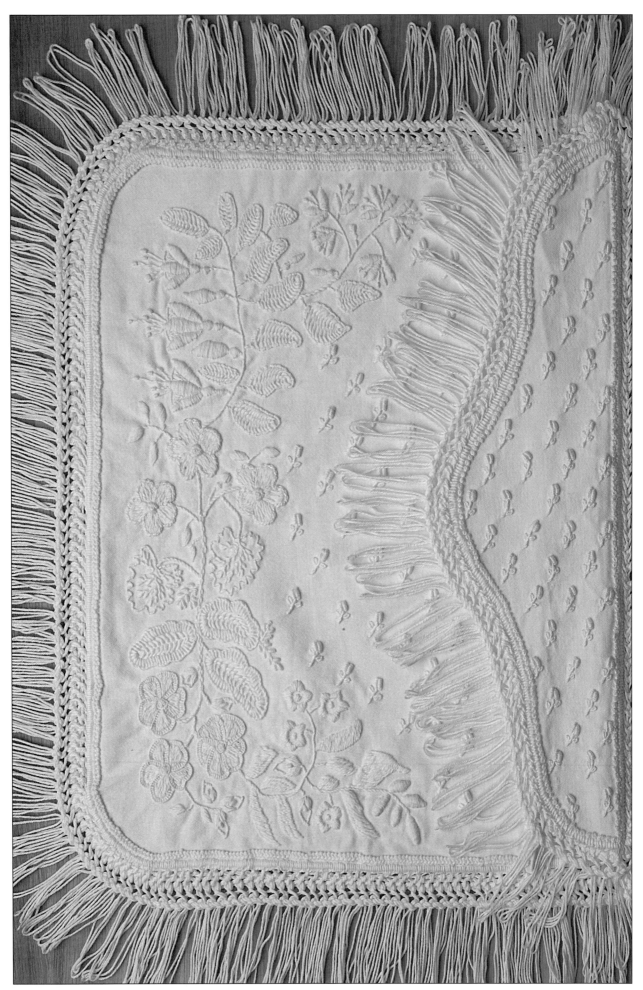

REPRODUCTION OF ANTIQUE NIGHTDRESS CASE

MORE TIPS

WORKING ROSES and DAISIES

These flowers are usually worked in padded Satin Stitch, on an emroidery ring. The stitch is not fanned out from the baseline (the centre of the flower), instead it is worked straight up and down. Always start the stitch at the centre of the baseline of a petal working from there to complete the left side, and then take the thread back to the starting point and work the right side. The baseline of the petal is always held straight in front of the worker at all times, and when you reach the end of the baseline start to work the bottom of the stitch going up the side of the petal. The top part of the stitch will also start to come down the side of the petal. Complete one petal at a time; if all the petals are padded at the start of working it is not always possible to clearly see the design line between the petals.

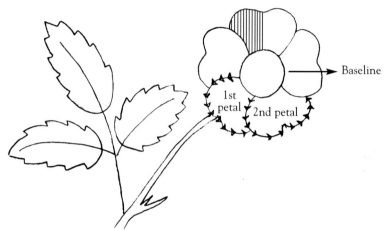

DEFINING SHAPES

The definition of some elements can be improved by where you start and finish your stitching. This is important when stitching a basket, bindweed buds and petals of flowers which share a design line and where the stitching used is defining the shape. Start stitching at the base of a petal and work as far as the outside point where the next petal joins the first one. Now start to work back up to this point from the base of the second petal. Continue around the design line to the point where the third petal meets the second and so on, continuing in this manner to complete the flower. Note the direction of the arrows on the lower petals on the diagram above.

SCATTERING

Scattering is an arrangement of Bullion Knots which are placed in an ordered pattern on a large item to fill an area between the main elements of the design. (See next page.) Draw lines vertically and horizontally over the area. Place the Bullion Knots alternating their positions on the lines (this is never worked until all the design embroidery is complete). Do not carry the thread across the back from one set of Bullions to another.

Redrawn from Pim patterns

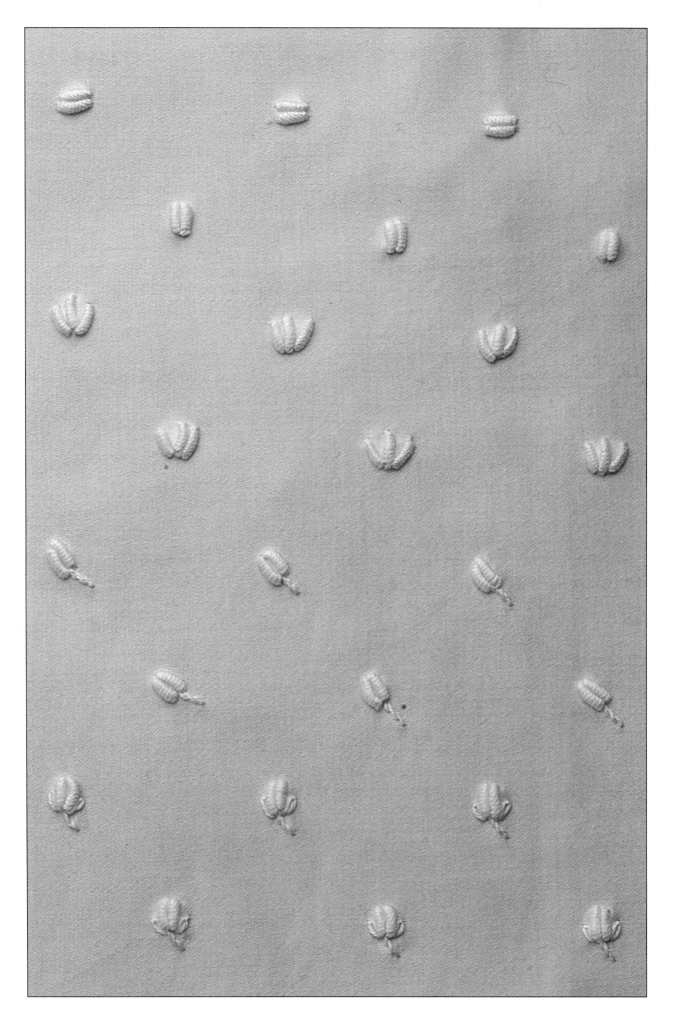

			METHOD 1[5] Two Bullion Knots = Grub Stitch		
			METHOD 2[9] Three Bullion Knots		
			METHOD 3[10] Two Bullion Knots + Stem Stitch		
			METHOD 4[9] Two Bullion Knots + Stem Stitch + Two Detached Chain (see pg 88)		
			METHOD 5[10] Four Detached Chain Stitches + French Knot		
		91			

DETAILS FROM ANTIQUE QUILTS

MAKING A BLACKBERRY

A blackberry is generally worked in French Knots. Using the following arrangement and work order will give the required effect. DO NOT leave a space between the knots, use the embroidery ring and check if the knot you are making is in the correct position before pulling through. No. 1 is the starting point in the centre of the blackberry.

Stage 1

Use three wraps of the needle and work in the following order 1–7

Stage 2

Use two wraps of the needle and work in the following order 8–13

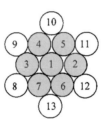

Stage 3

Use two wraps of the needle and work in the following order 14–19

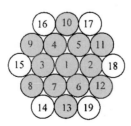

Redrawn from Pim patterns

Ideas for Use

Redrawn from Pim patterns

ANTIQUE WALL HANGING

ITEMS MADE

The following is a list of items that have been both made in the past and that are still being made today.

ANTIQUE

Bedspread, pillow sham [a rectangular piece to cover the pillows during the day], toilet cover [these were rectangular pieces which were draped on a chest of drawers, or the toilet table], brush and comb bag, night-dress case, tablecloths of all sizes, d'oiley and traycloths, runners, pram sham, handkerchief case, chair back covers, wall hanging, pin cushion and cot covers, some children's clothes and baby bibs, sometimes worked on a finer material.

MODERN

All off the above plus guest towel, drawstring toilet bag, pictures in box frames with coloured mounting, lamp shade and tablecloth with empty spaces for place settings, tablecloth with empty space in the centre for a vase, cushion cover, wedding ring cushion, waistcoat, fire screen, tea cosy and christening robes.

ANTIQUE WALL HANGING (pattern opposite)

JOY AND WOE	UNDER EVERY
ARE WOVEN FINE	GRIEF AND PINE
A CLOTHING FOR	RUNS A JOY
THE SOUL DIVINE	WITH SILKEN TWINE

Redrawn from Pim patterns

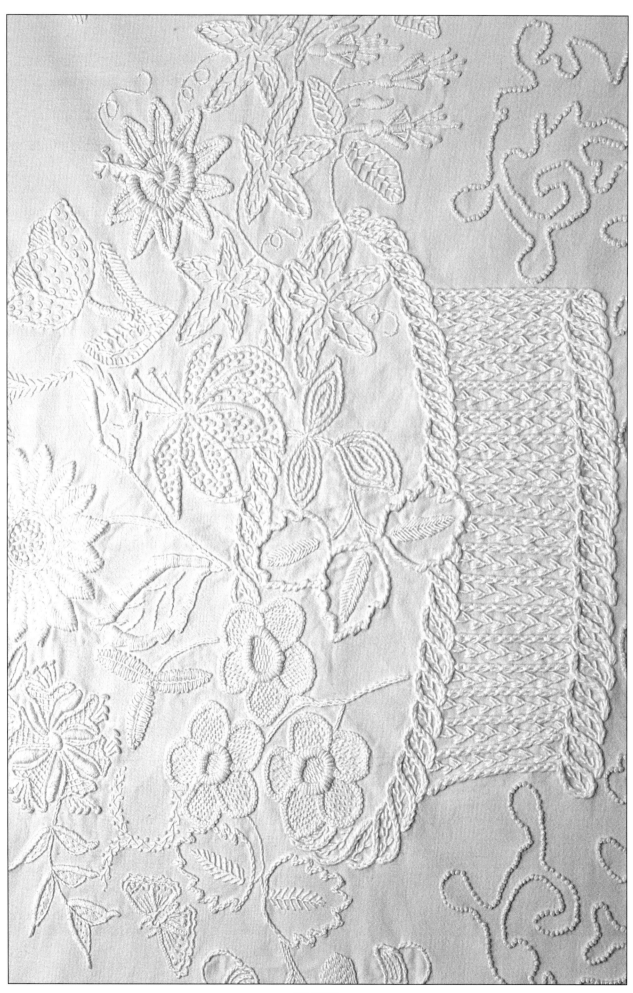

QUILT
CENTRAL PANEL, 1ST ELEMENT

QUILTS

CONSTRUCTION

A quilt is probably not the best name for this bedspread as it is neither padded or lined. It can be made in two ways:

1. By joining together squares of embroidered material to a required size, e.g. Weldons Practical Seventh series uses a pattern where the squares are 46cm and stitched together or joined using an unravelled knitted fringe. Today we would use the knitted fringe as an insert as on the circular cloth on pg 103.

2. Alternatively, cut a piece of the 137cm wide cotton satin to the required length of the bed, plus 60cm. This will form the central section for the quilt and should be embroidered before joining the side panels. Another length of fabric is cut the same length as the first and then cut in two, lengthways. This will form two side panels. The selvage edges of the side panels are then machined to the selvage edge of the central panel; make sure you stitch beyond the selvage itself. This will make a quilt which fits a double bed.

PATTERNS

- Are large and bold, you start in the centre with a floral element or with a monogram. Place only this pattern on the fabric when starting your quilt and subsequently place a complete pattern for each round only when required.
- The second element will surround the first; at this stage you may have to join on the side panels.
- This amount of fabric is not easy to handle. One way around this is to roll the fabric up to the working point from two directions. Using fishing line place ties at regular intervals along the length of the roll – the single entry of the fishing line into the fabric being so fine yet strong that it does not damage the fabric.
- Place a third element on the fabric.
- The fourth element is to fill the corners. On the example on page 101 a border was put on the quilt before working the fourth element, which included a seashell to fill right into the corner.

THREADS

Use a variety of thread thickness and pad well with knitting cotton; a light padding can also go under stitches like Cable Plait. The antique quilt in the An Grianan museum has a filler stitch which is worked in normal sewing thread.

FRINGES

A fringe is placed on the buttonhole edge around the quilt. There is no need to work the dropped part of the fringe at the head of the quilt. Knitting the fringe as usual with four strands of thread or 4ply knitting cotton and 15 stitches to a length to fit the sides and the bottom of the quilt. Start by sewing on at the top right hand corner of the quilt, attaching about 5cm down and leaving about 7cm of knitting free. This will allow movement for the grafting. When you get to the top left hand corner drop six stitches. DO NOT UNRAVEL. The unravelled fringe will make it harder to do the grafting. Continue to knit across the top of the quilt as usual, stitch this in position and then graft the two ends together. See Finishing Techniques for more on Fringes and Grafting.

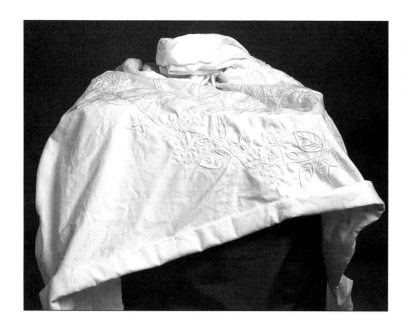

QUILT WORK IN PROGRESS
ROLLED and TIED WITH
FISHING LINE

QUILT 2ND ELEMENT

QUILT 3RD ELEMENT

QUILT 4TH ELEMENT

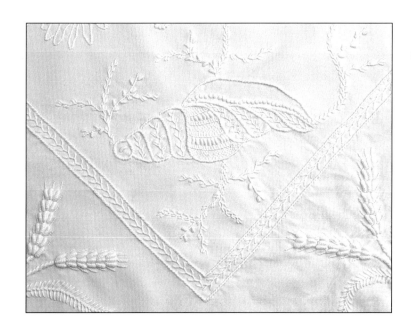

QUILT CORNER ELEMENT

QUILT BORDER ELEMENT

CIRCULAR TABLECLOTH

CIRCULAR TABLECLOTHS

CONSTRUCTION

To make a circular cloth without having a joining seam:

- The 137mm wide fabric will give a maximum working circle of 97cm and a drop of 16cm.
- Draw out the top circle on the fabric (plus 8cm to allow for shrinkage), then run a sewing tacking thread on the circle line. The marking ink can then be removed as otherwise it could be on the fabric a long time, depending on how extensive your embroidery is. Do not cut the circle out at this stage.
- On a second piece of fabric mark out a circle sized 8cm more than the diameter of the top (to allow for shrinkage), this will be the drop. A second circle is drawn approximately 20cm outside this circle or to the maximum the fabric will allow. Again remark with sewing tacking thread, do not cut what will be blank fabric in the centre of the circle until the embroidery is completed.
- Do not work the Buttonhole hem on the cloth top until you have checked the position of the markings against the table. If the cloth is for a specific table it would be worth laundering the top before placing the Buttonhole edging, though this does make stitching through the fabric difficult. The inner and outer edge of the drop can be stitched before laundering, but if the top has been laundered it is best to also do the drop before joining the two together. Cut the fabric in the usual way after the buttonholing is completed. If this is cut with care you will have another circle of fabric to make a smaller cloth.
- The insertion which joins the two sections together will stretch to accommodate the larger circumference of the drop to fit the smaller circumference of the top.

THE INSERTION[14]

Knit a two strand fringe using six stitches, take care not to stretch the work while knitting. Stitch to the cloth top first making sure it is well packed in. Stitch the drop to the insertion, and put a normal six stitch knitted fringe on the bottom.

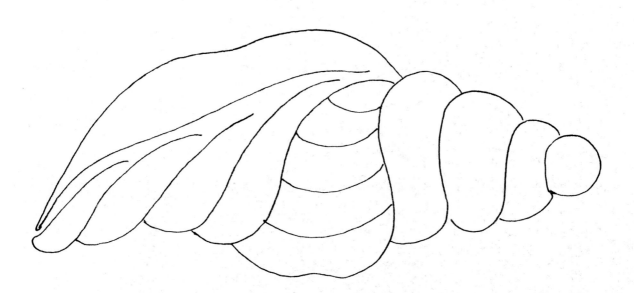

TABLECLOTH with PLACE SETTINGS

TABLECLOTHS with PLACE SETTINGS

A tablecloth with no embroidery under the place settings is a very useable cloth, and as such allows the beauty of the cloth to be seen. Start by preparing the fabric as normal, then place it on the table and lay the plates etc. in their usual positions. Do not forget the centre, e.g. flower container, condiments and serving dishes. Mark out around these positions with the water soluble pen. Replace these markings with a sewing thread tacking, soak off the soluble pen. Design your pattern to flow around the settings. On a large cloth extra fabric may be required for the drop; follow the instructions for the circular cloth. Joins in the drop fabric are inevitable so try to use the selvage for the joins. Working a piece this size can be awkward so tie up with fishing line. [See Quilts, pg 99.]

TABLECLOTH with PLACE SETTINGS
WORK IN PROGRESS

LAMPSHADE

LAMPSHADES

The frame used for a lampshade should not have too many curves or bends on it, try to have one which is plastic coated. This means the shade can be washed without removing it from the frame.

- Make a pattern of each panel from the frame on to greaseproof paper, and mark it out on to the fabric. Allow plenty of spare material when cutting the fabric as there will be shrinkage. Do not machine stitch the panels together until the embroidery is laundered, then tack the panels together to fit the frame.
- After machine stitching, overlock or Buttonhole the seams with sewing thread and iron them open. Place the fabric over the frame and pin the top into position. The bottom of the shade is now stretched and pinned onto the frame. Overstitch with strong white sewing thread the fabric to the frame both top and bottom. This may need to be repeated to get the tension right. Buttonhole stitch the top and bottom of the frame and then trim the excess material.
- The top of the shade can be finished with a 2 strand, 3 stitch, knitted fringe worked on small needles. This will produce a narrow band which can be stitched on top of the Buttonholing. [The Buttonholing must be worked under the band as it will stop the fabric fraying.] A 2 or 3 strand, 6 stitch, knitted fringe, giving a 3 stitch drop, is placed on the bottom.
- Great care needs to be taken while doing the embroidery that NO threads cross the back of the work, as these will show through when the light is turned on.

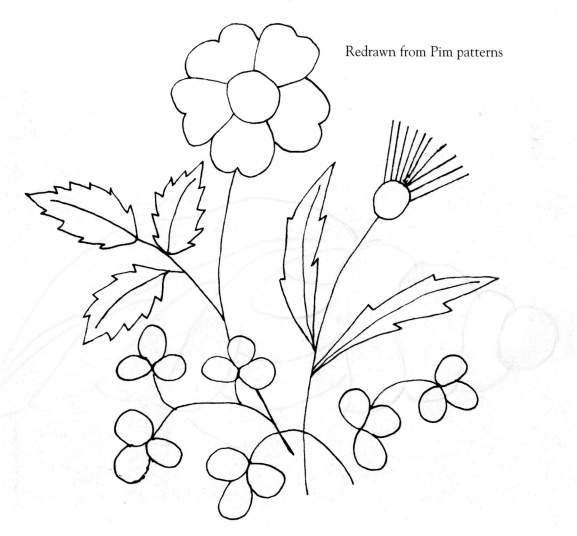

Redrawn from Pim patterns

107

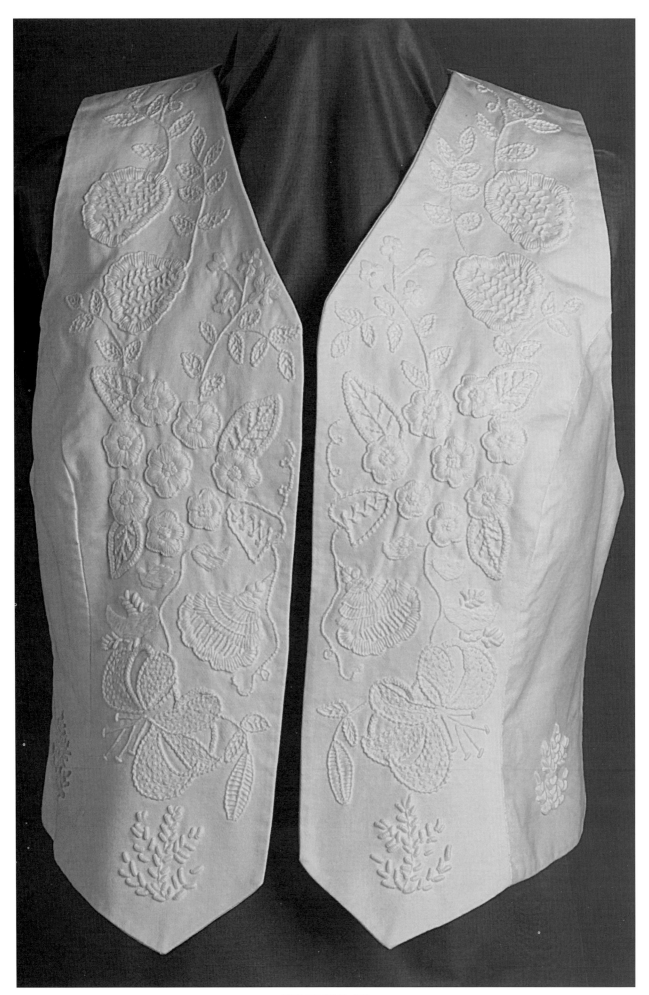

WAISTCOAT

WAISTCOATS

- A dress-making pattern for a five-panel waistcoat avoids the problem of having darts.
- DO NOT cut out the panels to the pattern. Mark out the panels onto the fabric with the water soluble pen, and then with a sewing tacking thread.
- Cut the fabric, being very generous with the amount.
- Soak overnight in cold water to remove the pen markings and then place your embroidery pattern within the confines of the tacking thread.
- Work the embroidery and when completed remove the tacking thread and launder. Now make up the waistcoat as normal, and line with a fine cotton.

WAISTCOAT BACK

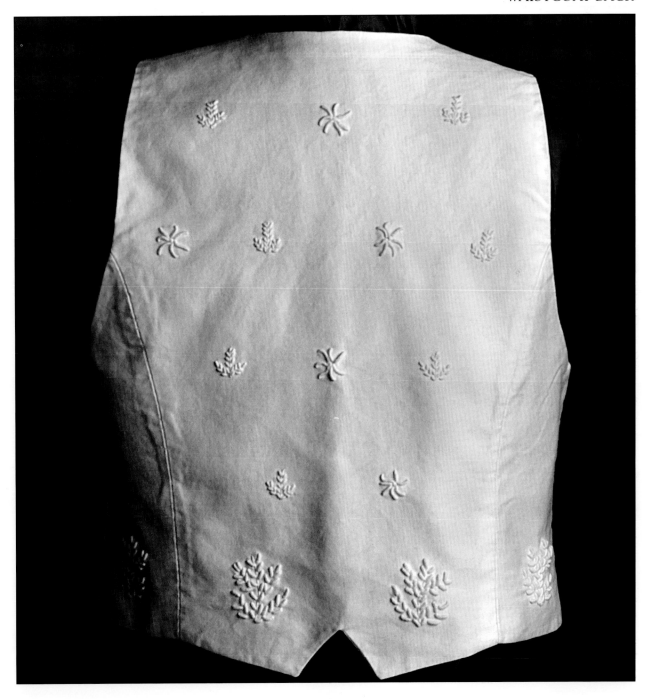

WEDDING RING CUSHION

WEDDING RING CUSHIONS

A wedding ring cushion is a very unusual way to show off your talents, and it makes a lovely memento of the day.

- The cushion can be circular or square.
- On the back embroider the couple's initials and the wedding date.
- On the front centre place a Bullion Knot that is removed later. The ribbon to tie the rings on the cushion is threaded through this Bullion. Make sure a guest has a pair of scissors to hand just in case the ribbon is pulled into a knot and has to be cut.

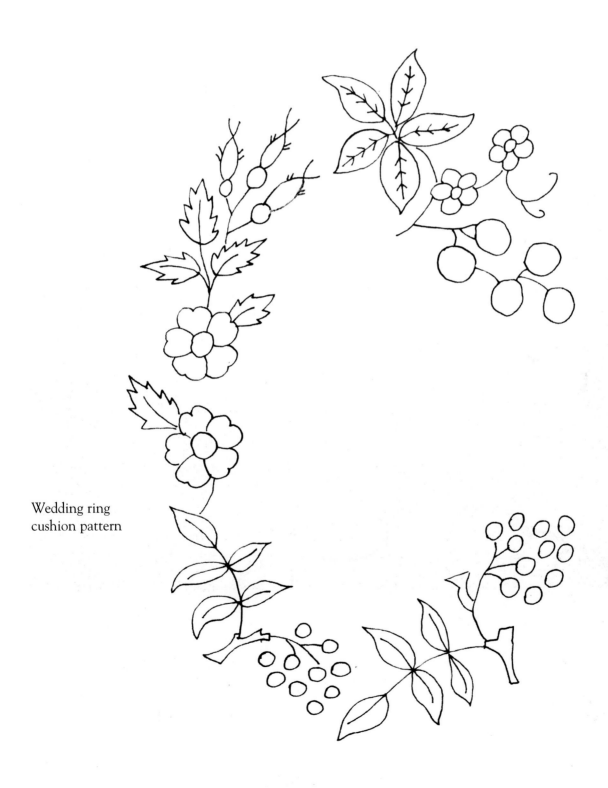

Wedding ring
cushion pattern

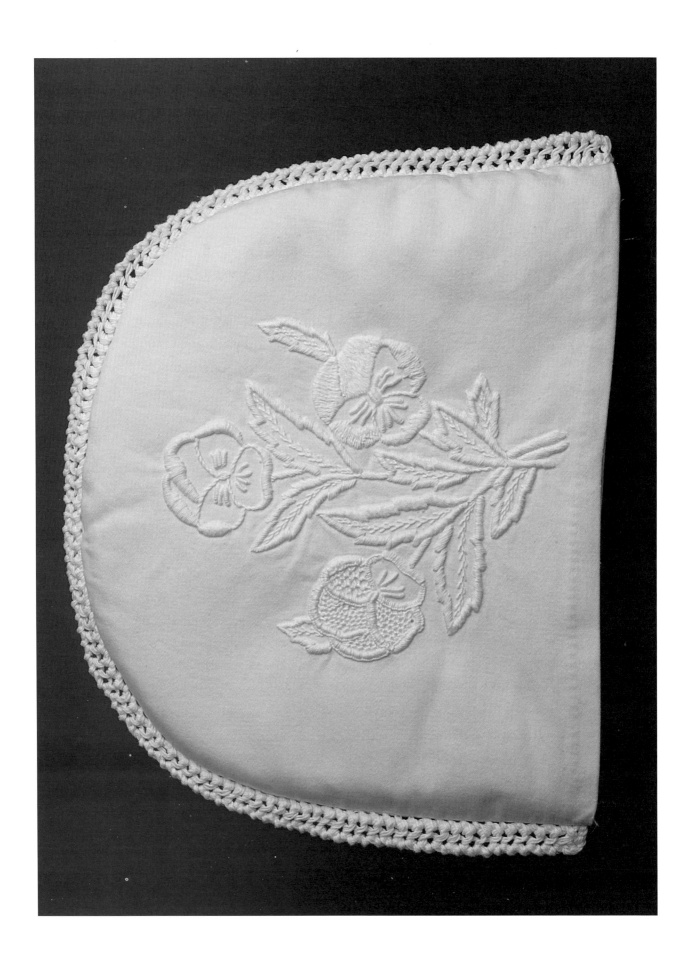

TEA COSY

TEA COSIES

Make the tea cosy to fit a pre-bought or homemade pad as it has to be a detachable cover for laundering and so the fit needs to be exact.

- Trace the outline of the pad twice onto the fabric and work a pattern on each piece.
- Launder the work before retracing the pad onto the fabric and then machine-join the two halves together. Now trim the fabric.
- Try to use the fabric selvage at the open end as then you will only need a single turn-in for the hem. A double turn-under on a raw edge will make the hem very bulky. Work a slip stitch along the hem.
- Knit a two-strand, three-stitch fringe pattern as a braid and stitch this around the cosy.

CELTIC DESIGN of DOG

CELTIC DOGS

This dog is worked as a picture. He is stiched in Indian Filler, French Knots, Satin and Whipped Chain Stitch.

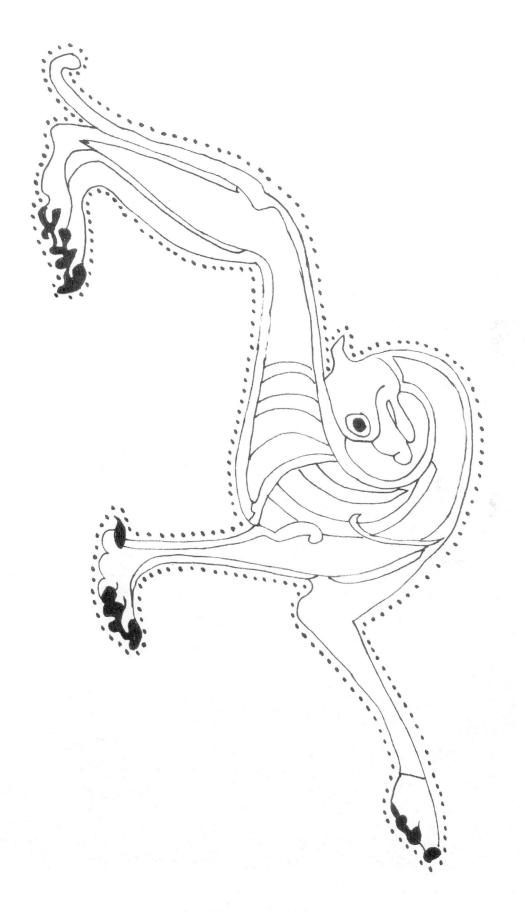

Pattern continues on next page

Finishing Techniques

Redrawn from Pim Patterns

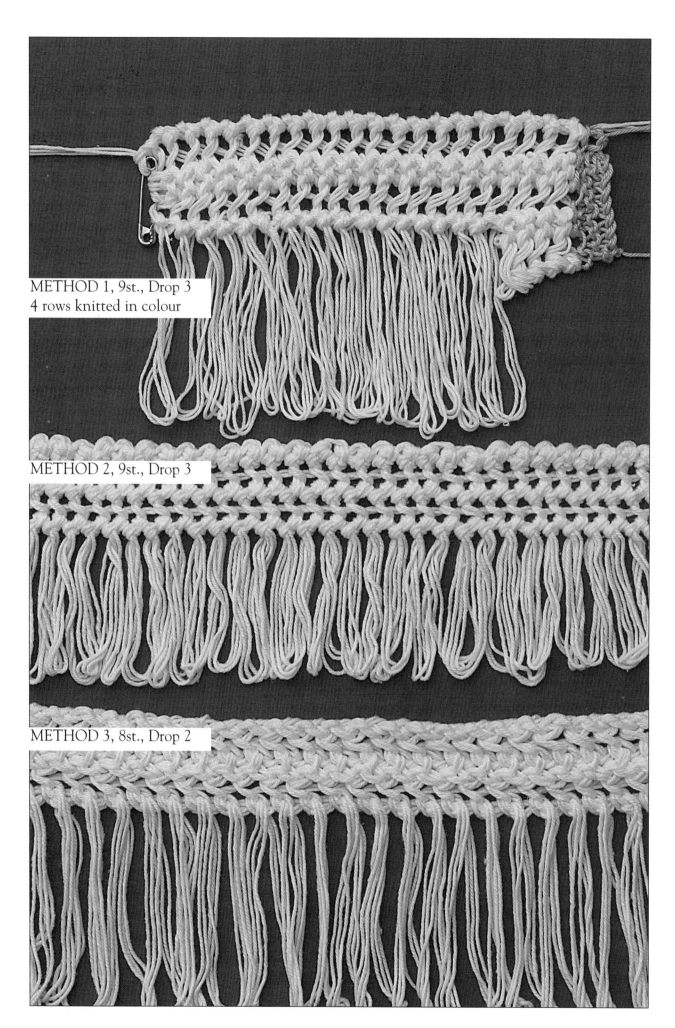

METHOD 1, 9st., Drop 3
4 rows knitted in colour

METHOD 2, 9st., Drop 3

METHOD 3, 8st., Drop 2

118

KNITTED FRINGES

Traditionally Mountmellick Work has a knitted fringe trim, although a few antique pieces have other types such as knitted lace, machine made lace, Bobbin lace or crochet.

FRINGE

- The fringe is made by knitting a lace as follows and on completion a number of stitches are dropped and unravelled.
- Make a set of samples of about 20 rows, on different size needles, with different numbers of stitches for future reference.
- Take care that all threads pass around the needle while knitting.
- Needle size: 2.75, 3 or 3.25mm (short metal needles are easier to work with).
- Thread: 2, 3 or 4 strands of the main thread used in the embroidery.

Method 1

- Cast on stitches in multiples of three (the most common being nine). Start with the coloured knitting cotton. Work 4 rows of plain knitting, then change to your white thread.
- 1st Row: *Knit 1, make 1, knit 2 together*. Repeat to the end.
  2nd and subsequent rows: Repeat as in row one. DO NOT CAST OFF
- When you think you have sufficient length, start to stitch the fringe onto the embroidery.
- Make sure all knitting joining threads are at the fabric edge, so they can be woven in later.
- You will always have to knit some extra rows. DO NOT STRETCH THE KNITTING.

ATTACHING FRINGE

- Trim the fabric of the embroidery back to 3cm from the buttonhole edge.
- Stitch the top loop of the knitting to the base bar of the Buttonhole Stitch edge with a slip stitch using the embroidery thread. DO NOT START ON A CORNER OR ENTER THE FABRIC.
- Start stitching about 5cm from the start of the lace knitting. Make sure you pack the lace in when going around a corner. Knit any extra rows which may be required, finishing at the fabric side. Do not sew the last 5cm to the fabric until the ends are joined together.

JOINING THE ENDS

Cut through the coloured cotton, remove the threads and pick up the white stitches onto your second knitting needle. Graft the two ends of the lace together (fig. 1) starting at the fabric end. See Grafting, pg 121.

Antique linen
quilt monogram

119

FIG. 1. METHOD 1
9st., cut coloured thread

FIG. 2. GRAFTING

GRAFTING

Cut the knitting threads leaving about 30cm for the grafting. Thread all 3 cut threads on to a large tapestry needle (fig. 1). Place the knitting needles together parallel and hold both in your left hand (fig. 2). When pulling through the sewing thread, keep the tension loose. The following method is for a fringe worked in knit stitch. If purl is used reverse the grafting to purl wise.

1. Pass the sewing needle into the 1st stitch, front knitting needle, knit wise. Pull through and slip this stitch off the knitting needle.
2. Pass the sewing needle into the 1st stitch, back knitting needle, knit wise. Pull through and slip this stitch off the knitting needle (Fig.2).
3. Pass the sewing needle into the next two stitches, front knitting needle, knit wise. Pull through and slip these two stitches off the knitting needle.
4. Pass the sewing needle into the next two stitches, back knitting needle, knit wise. Pull through and slip these two stitches off the knitting needle.
5. Repeat from 1 until the number of stitches left are the number you want to drop, e.g. 3 on each knitting needle. Remove the knitting needles.
6. Place the graft on a firm surface and tension the sewing thread to match up the lace. Pass the sewing needle again through the last stitch worked on the front knitting needle, pull through leaving a loop, slip the sewing needle through this loop and pull through.
7. Remove the sewing needle. Do not cut the excess thread until the fringe is pulled. Return now to stitching the fringe to your piece, and weave in all threads.
8. Unravel the dropped stitches starting at what would have been the cast off end (it will not unravel from the cast on end).
9. Trim the excess fabric and launder the piece.

NOTES
1. When joining in new threads in the fringe stagger their introduction and keep them all on the same side of the knitting as the starting thread.
2. Do not knot on new threads, just feed them in at the start of a row leaving about 10cm of old thread and the same of new. This will allow sufficient thread to weave in later.
3. When knitting with three strands the threads can get tangled, prevent this as follows: place the balls of thread in a drawstring bag, pass the three threads through the centre of the empty cotton reel, close the bag and leaving the reel on the outside, join the thread to the knitting. The thread will feed through the top of the closed bag and will not tangle as you work.

TRIMMING THE FABRIC

Trim the fabric from the front of the embroidery by holding the lace and fringe back on top of the fabric with your left thumb and exposing the raw edge. With the nail scissors snip the fabric very carefully all around, leaving about 1cm of fabric. This fabric will fray back over time and washing to the buttonhole edge. NEVER pull these threads away, cut when required.

Pattern from antique sampler

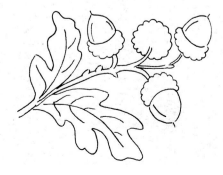

CLOTH with VASE SPACE

OTHER PATTERNS

Method 2
All the knitting can be done in purl stitch using Method 1. See page 118.

Method 3
Seen on an antique piece. See page 118.
- Cast on the required number of stitches in multiples of 2.
- 1st row: *yarn round needle, knit 2 together*. Repeat to end.
- 2nd row: Knit to end.
- Repeat these two rows.

Method 4
Seen on an antique piece, this method is best suited for a quilt.
- Cast on 8–10 stitches and use 6mm needles.
- All rows are the same: *yarn round needle, slip 1, knit 1, pass the slip stitch over*.
- Repeat to the end.

METHOD 4
8st., DROP 2

ANTIQUE SAMPLER

LAUNDRY

Do not worry if the embroidery is looking grubby, this is going to happen especially if working on a large piece, and we are very lucky that the fabric we use can be boiled. Never iron your embroidery while work is in progress as this may fix the pattern on the fabric. If you are using a water soluble pen and you have a stain caused by exposure to sunlight, heat, not having soaked before washing or even the fact that the design has been on for a long period of time, with care it can be removed. Test the stain remover on a sample piece first: boil the sample with some marker pen on it, dry and then, following the manufacturer's instructions, remove the yellow stain. Try Stain Devil remover – for iron mould, I have found this works well but you must wash the embroidery well between each application.

1. Soak the finished work overnight in cold water.
2. Wash in soap flakes (such as Lux) or non-biological washing powder. Cotton is a natural fibre so enzymes in biological detergents will break down the fibres of the cotton over the years.
3. As with all 100% cottons the embroidery can be boiled to whiten it. Add a small amount of soap flakes to the water, allow it to heat up and dissolve the soap. Add the embroidery, bring to the boil and remove from the heat after a few minutes, drain and refill with warm water and bring again to the boil for a few minutes without soaps flakes. Repeat until all traces of soap are gone. Rinse until water runs clear.
4. Dry naturally.
5. Steam iron the embroidery face down on several layers of towels. This will raise the stitches from the surface.
6. Never use starch: it is not necessary, it will clog the fringe and over time it will damage the fabric.

Patterns from antique sampler

CARE of ANTIQUE PIECES

CLEANING

Wash by hand in warm soap flakes, do not try to remove stains or to boil. A lot of old items are a grey colour, you should not try to whiten them. The final two rinses should be with spring or distilled water. Dry naturally away from direct sunlight. Store, rolled in acid free tissue paper, if possible have no folds in the embroidery.

REPAIRING

It is best not to try and repair an antique piece, support any major damage as follows:
Make a patch larger than the tear or hole by overlocking a piece of fabric, which has been laundered. Using white sewing cotton and a small running stitch working from the front, attach the patch to the back of the piece and then, with a few small stitches also on the front, catch down the raw edges of the damage.

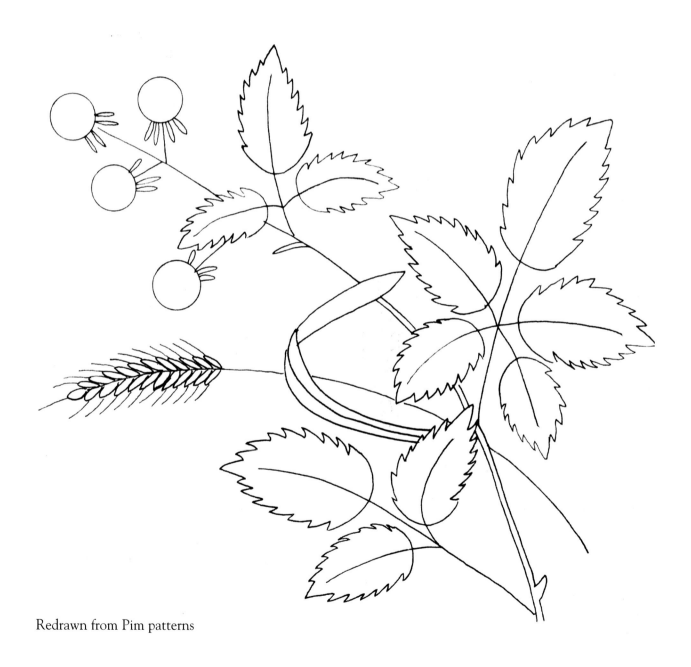

Redrawn from Pim patterns

SUPPLIERS

IRELAND AND UK

Fabric: Whaleys [Bradford] Ltd, Harris Court, Great Horton, Bradford, West Yorkshire, BD7 4EQ, England. Tel: +44 [0]1274 576718 Fax: +44 [0]1274 521309.
E-mail: whaleys@btinternet.com Web: www.whaleys.bradford.ltd.uk
Also suppliers of other craft fabrics.

Thread: Craftspun Yarns, Rathmore, Naas, County Kildare, Ireland.
Tel: +353 [0]45 862966. E-mail: craftspun@eircom.net Web: www.knitting-wools.com

The list below is not a recommendation of quality.

CANADA

Fabric and Thread: Tanja Berlin, Berlin Embroidery Designs, 1481 Hunterbrook Road NW, Calgary, Alberta T2K 4V4, Canada. Tel: +1 [403] 274 6293
E-mail: tanja@berlinembroidery.com Web: www.berlinembroidery.com

NORTH AMERICA

Fabric and Thread: Jenny June Fancy Work, PO Box 367, Randolph, V.T. 05060, U.S.A.
Tel. +1 [800] 715 3558 E-mail: jenny@jennyjune.com Web: www.jennyjune.com

WHERE TO SEE MOUNTMELLICK WORK

Mountmellick Development Association Museum (dedicated to Mountmellick embroidery)
Irishtown, Mountmellick, County Laois, Ireland.
Tel: +353 [0] 502 24525 Email: mdaltd@indigo.ie

The National Museum of Ireland
Collins Barracks, Benburb Street, Dublin 7, Ireland. Tel: +353 [0]1 6777444
Fax: +353 [0]1 6777828 Email: marketing@museum.ie Web: www.museum.ie

An Grianan Adult Education College, Termonfeckin, County Louth, Ireland
Tel: +353 [0]41 982 2119 Fax: +353 [0]41 982 2690 E mail: admin@an-grianan.ie Web: www.ica.ie

Muckross House, Killarney, County Kerry, Ireland
Tel: +353 [0]64 31440 Fax: +353 [0]64 33926 Email: mucros@iol.ie Web: www.muckross-house.ie

The Ulster Folk and Transport Museum.
Cultra, Holywood, County Down, BT18 0EU, Northern Ireland. Tel: +44 [0]28 9042 8428
Fax: +44 [0]28 9042 8728 Email: uftm@talk21.com Web: www.nidex.com/uftm/index.htm

The Victoria and Albert Museum.
Cromwell Road, South Kensington, London SW7 2RL, England. Tel: +44 [0] 20 7942 2680
Email: textilesandfashion@vam.ac.uk Web: www.vam.ac.uk

* Four weeks notice is required to view items at most venues.

NOTES

1. Weldons Practical Mountmellick Embroidery, 1st Series, c.1886.
2. Weldons Practical Mountmellick Embroidery, 5th Series.
3. Weldons Practical Mountmellick Embroidery, 6th Series.
4. Weldons Practical Mountmellick Embroidery, 7th Series.
5. Weldons Practical Mountmellick Embroidery, 8th Series.
6. *Needlecraft Practical Journal Mountmellick Embroidery*, No. 108 (Wm. Briggs & Co. Ltd, Manchester: c.1913).
7. *The Delineator*, April 1904, USA.
8. *Mrs Leach's Practical Fancy Work Basket*, No. 55, April 1890.
9. As seen on antique piece of embroidery.
10. As seen on antique piece of embroidery in the National Museum of Ireland.
11. As seen on antique quilt in An Grianan Museum.
12. *The Quakers of Mountmellick* (FAS: 1994).
13. Houston-Almquist, Jane, *Mountmellick Work, Irish White Embroidery* (Dolmen Press).
14. *The Priscilla Needlework Book* (Priscilla Publishing Co., USA: 1904).
15. *Home Needlework Magazine*, Vol. 2, No. 4, October 1900, USA.
16. Annals of the Presentation Convent, Mountmellick (not published).

FURTHER READING

Annals of the Presentation Convent, Mountmellick (not published).

Beale, Edgar, *The Earth Between Them* (Westworth Books Sydney: 1975), ISBN O-85587-081-8

Gifford, M.K., *The Hobby Book: Needlework*, c.1911.

Houston-Almquist, Jane, *Mountmellick Work, Irish White Embroidery* (Dolmen Press), ISBN O-85105-512-5.

Kliot, Jules & Kaethe, *Mountmellick Embroidery* (Lacis Pub, California: 1998), ISBN O-916896-94-3 (contains Weldons Practical Needlework 1st–7th series and Priscilla Needlework Book for 1904).

Needlecraft Practical Journal Mountmellick Embroidery, No. 108 (Wm. Briggs & Co. Ltd, Manchester: c.1913).

The Irish Flowerer (Institute of Irish Studies Q.U.B & Ulster Folk Museum: 1971).

The Priscilla Needlework Book (Priscilla Publishing Co., USA: 1904).

The Quakers of Mountmellick (FAS: 1994), ISBN 0-86335-008-9.

Thomas, Mary, *Mary Thomas' Embroidery Book* (Hodder & Stoughton: 1936).

Townend, Mrs B., *Talks on Art Needlework*, c.1905.

Weldons Encyclopaedia (The Waverley Book Co.: c.1900).

Weldons Practical Mountmellick Embroidery, 1st Series, c.1886.

Weldons Practical Mountmellick Embroidery, 5th–8th Series.

PAMPHLETS AND MAGAZINES

Home Needlework Magazine, Vol. 2, No. 4, October 1900, USA.

Home Needlework Magazine, Vol. 3, No. 4, October 1901, USA.

Mrs Leach's Practical Fancy Work Basket, No. 55, April 1890.

The Delineator, April, May and June 1904, USA.

Weldons Practical Guide to Fancy Work – Mountmellick, 1922

Weldons Practical Shilling Guide to Fancy Work – Mountmellick Work.

Redrawn from Pim patterns

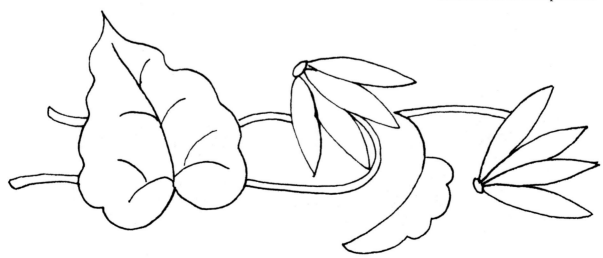

Redrawn from Pim patterns

Redrawn from Pim patterns

Redrawn from Pim patterns